LINCOLN CHRISTIAN COLLEGE

P9-DFC-512

SCIENCE
HELD
HOSTAGE

What's Wrong with Creation Science *AND* Evolutionism

Howard J. Van Till/ Davis A. Young/ Clarence Menninga

INTERVARSITY PRESS
DOWNERS GROVE, ILLINOIS 60515

© 1988 by the Calvin Center for Christian Scholarship

All rights reserved. No part of this book may be reproduced in any form without written permission from InterVarsity Press, P.O. Box 1400, Downers Grove, Illinois 60515.

InterVarsity Press is the book-publishing division of InterVarsity Christian Fellowship, a student movement active on campus at hundreds of universities, colleges and schools of nursing. For information about local and regional activities, write Public Relations Dept., InterVarsity Christian Fellowship, 6400 Schroeder Rd., P.O. Box 7895, Madison, WI 53707-7895.

Distributed in Canada through InterVarsity Press, 860 Denison St., Unit 3, Markham, Ontario L3R 4H1, Canada.

Cover illustration: Guy Wolek

ISBN 0-8308-1253-9

Printed in the United States of America

Library of Congress Cataloging in Publication Data

Van Till, Howard, 1938—
Science held hostage.

Bibliography: p.
1. Creationism.   2. Evolution.   3. Science—
Methodology.   4. Religion and science—1946-
I. Title.
BS651.V35   1988   501   88-8810
ISBN 0-8308-1253-9

| 17 | 16 | 15 | 14 | 13 | 12 | 11 | 10 | 9 | 8 | 7 | 6 | 5 | 4 | 3 | 2 |
| 99 | 98 | 97 | 96 | 95 | 94 | 93 | 92 | 91 | 90 | 89 | 88 |

Preface

This book is a product of research and writing begun while the authors were fellows of the Calvin Center for Christian Scholarship (CCCS) at Calvin College, Grand Rapids, Michigan. We are deeply grateful for that opportunity to work as a community of Christian scholars, and we hereby express our gratitude not only to the governing board of the CCCS, but also to the many persons whose financial support has made possible this continuing program of Christian scholarship.

Each of the three authors of this work is responsible for specific chapters. Chapters four and five were written by Clarence Menninga; chapters six and seven were written by Davis A. Young; the remainder were written by Howard J. Van Till, who also served as the editor for this collaborative volume and as the coordinator for the 1984-85 CCCS study on the topic "Creation and Cosmogony."

As authors of this work we wish to acknowledge the helpful insights contributed by our colleagues, especially those who served with us as fellows on this study project: Prof. John Stek of Calvin Theological Seminary; Prof. Robert E. Snow of the State University College of Arts and Science at Potsdam, New York; the Rev. John Suk, who served while a student at Calvin Theological Seminary; and Prof. George M. Marsden, now at the Divinity School, Duke University. We also wish to thank Ellen Alderink, Calvin College Audio-Visual Department, for rendering the figures in chapter six.

Finally, our thanks to Mr. James Hoover and his colleagues at InterVarsity Press for their cheerful assistance in taking this book from manuscript to finished product.

Grand Rapids
February 1988

Howard J. Van Till
Davis A. Young
Clarence Menninga

82834

83.534

INTRODUCTION: CHARTING THE COURSE

NATURAL SCIENCE TEXTBOOKS OFTEN INCLUDE AN introductory chapter on "the nature of science" or "the scientific method." That's not a bad idea—something like consulting a road map before venturing on a cross-country trip. But the content of these textbook introductions often leaves much to be desired.

Perhaps such shortcomings only indicate a larger problem. Though we live within a culture that has been extensively influenced by modern natural science, the scientific enterprise is still misunderstood by many persons—even by educators and scientists themselves. The revival of the creation-evolution controversy provides ample evidence that serious misunderstanding exists. And this dispute, as it is ordinarily carried on, is but one specific manifestation of a more widespread perception that science and religion are (or should be) engaged in some sort of warfare.

We strongly contest that perception. We judge that the warfare metaphor, which characterizes the relationship between science and religion in terms of fierce competition for a common territory, promotes a gross misperception of that relationship. Properly understood, we believe, the two are not enemies, but partners in the quest for understanding ourselves and our world.[1]

The goal of this book is modest. We seek to challenge some of the misperceptions concerning the nature of the professional scientific enterprise, and to illustrate the mischief that flows from these misperceptions by presenting case studies drawn principally from the arena of the creation-evolution debate.

In discussing the nature of the scientific enterprise we will be very selective. For example, we will say relatively little about the "scientific method," and we will make no attempt to develop sharp distinctions among terms like *hypothesis, theory, model* and *law*. Instead, our chief concerns will be: (1) to identify the accepted *domain* of professional natural science; and (2) to give due recognition to the system of *values* which function within the professional scientific community. We believe that much of the antagonism and mistrust associated with the creation-evolution debate could be dispelled if both of the disputing parties would learn to recognize the distinction between the scientific and religious domains of concern, and if both parties would abide by the system of values that have developed within the professional scientific community.

Following our discussions of domain and values, we will present a number of case studies that will illustrate what happens when either of these two concepts is disregarded. And going beyond illustration, we will take *evolutionary naturalism* to task for its failure to honor the accepted boundaries of the scientific domain, and we will criticize *scientific creationism* chiefly for its failure to employ an appropriate system of values in the construction and evaluation of scientific theories.*

Before we proceed, however, we should clarify our understanding of the term *natural sciences* and the object of their investigation. Our goal here is not to present some novel or unusual twist, but only to be clear in identifying the generally accepted meanings of these concepts.

By *natural sciences* we simply mean those endeavors known by such names as astronomy, biology, chemistry, geology and physics, along with their subdivisions and the numerous related or combined disciplines. (In order to limit the scope of our discussion we choose not to consider the social sciences or other disciplines concerned with human *personal* behavior.) The natural sciences are closely interrelated, and the borders between them are somewhat fuzzy and subject to change. The present boundaries between the several sciences could be seen by perusing the subject matter treated in the professional scientific journals. But we are not concerned, at the moment, with these subdivisions, and we prefer to speak collectively of the entire family of natural sciences.

What does this family of investigative disciplines study? What is the *object* that is investigated by the natural sciences? To these questions we give a very direct answer: the object of study by the natural sciences is the *physical universe,* no more, no less. It is the world of atoms and the subatomic particles comprising them. It is the world of things

---

* By *naturalism* we mean that philosophical and religious perspective which is based on the assumption that the physical world is all there is, that there exists no divine being capable of influencing physical phenomena. And by *evolutionary naturalism* we mean that form of naturalism which claims that the scientific concept of evolution provides a sufficient basis for rejecting the idea of divine governance of natural processes.

By *scientific creationism* we mean that perspective which proceeds from the claim that it is possible to employ the results of natural science to demonstrate that the universe was recently created in a mature and fully functioning form; that is, that the religiously derived concept of special creation can be validated by the results of scientific investigation.

made of atoms: of molecules, rocks, stars, galaxies, living cells, plants and animals. Whatever can fruitfully be viewed as a physical system—a set of mutually interacting physical entities—can be the object of investigation by the natural sciences.

Nonphysical things are not the object of study by these sciences. The natural sciences in no way deny the existence of other realms of reality; they merely choose to restrict their attention to the physical realm alone. In large part this restriction of the object of study is a consequence of a restriction in the method of acquiring information. Modern natural science is inextricably associated with the empirical, that is, observational, approach. The object of scientific investigation must be empirically accessible—there must be some way to interact with it physically. Anything that is empirically inaccessible, that provides no avenue of physical interaction, cannot function as the object of study by the natural sciences. The nonphysical realm—an important realm indeed—must be investigated by other means.

These restrictions in the object of investigation, the sources of information and the methods of data gathering and analysis are not the product of some externally imposed force. Rather they are the result of how the professional scientific community has developed. They are time-tested choices that have demonstrated their fruitfulness.

SCIENCE AS
PRACTICED
BY SCIENTISTS
PART I

The practices of natural science are not established by either legal decree or logical necessity. Rather, they grow out of the collective experience of the scientific community. In this section we focus our attention on two products of this experience. First, we look at what have become generally accepted as the boundaries of the *domain* of natural science—the restricted categories of questions that it chooses to address. Second, we look at the system of *values* that functions within the professional scientific community as it performs its empirical investigation and as it constructs and evaluates explanatory theories.

LOCATING
THE
BOUNDARY
1

ALTHOUGH THE ENTIRE PHYSICAL UNIVERSE MAY BE the *object* of investigation by the natural sciences, not all of its attributes fall within the *domain* of scientific inquiry. But before we approach this matter formally, let's illustrate the distinction between object and domain with an example that is close at hand.

The words that appear on this page are formed by a particular distribution of ink on paper. Employing all of the tools of natural science we may be able to determine the identity and (within certain limits) the location of every atom comprising this printed page. But this scientific description of the spatial distribution of atoms would be notably incomplete. It would, no matter how complete from the standpoint of natural science, still fail to reveal an authentic and important feature of this page—the fact that this particular distribution of atoms and molecules forms words, and that these words convey a certain message.

Natural science is an appropriate and powerful tool for investigating and gaining knowledge about the physical features of the object of its study, but is wholly incapable of discovering its *meaning*. Consequently, to say that this page is nothing but a particular assembly of atoms and molecules, or to assert that the physical universe is "all there is or ever was or ever will be" is to speak nonsense.[1] Donald MacKay, in *The Clockwork Image*, calls this nonsense by the colorful but appropriate name "nothing buttery."[2]

Furthermore, to assert that natural science is capable of answering all meaningful questions about reality or that only those questions answerable by natural science are truly meaningful is also nonsense. Such outlandish assertions are not claims made by natural science itself; they are the philosophical-religious assertions of what is better known as *scientism*. To have a healthy respect for what we can learn by studying the world of atoms and molecules is good science, but to claim that natural science is the only path to knowledge or that it is applicable to everything is an arrogant expression of scientism. The distinction between science and scientism ought never to be overlooked.

The Questions Natural Science Addresses
Speaking more formally now, to identify the *domain* of natural science is to identify the categories of questions that it is capable of addressing. As our example of the printed page has illustrated, the natural sciences are not capable of dealing with all conceivable questions about a physical object; only certain categories of questions lie within its domain. We shall approach the matter of identifying the boundary of this domain by citing several additional examples of questions that clearly lie within the scientific domain and then noting the categories into which these questions naturally fit. We will, of course, keep in

mind that these must all be questions about the proper object of scientific investigation—the physical universe and its constituent parts.

What is the surface temperature of the star Betelgeuse? What is the value of the proton mass? What is the structure of a DNA molecule? All of these are appropriate questions for scientific investigation. Each of them fits into the category of questions concerning the *physical properties* of physical objects. All questions that fit into this category, we believe, lie within the domain of natural science.

Consider another family of questions: What physical process is responsible for maintaining the surface temperature of Betelgeuse? What takes place when an acid and a base are combined? What occurs in the process of photosynthesis? These, too, are questions that the natural sciences are capable of investigating. Each of these questions fits squarely within the general category of questions concerning the *physical behavior* of some physical system, and, as such, it lies within the domain of natural science. As a matter of fact, one of the major endeavors in natural science is to construct adequate and accurate descriptions of such phenomena and to discover the universally applicable patterns of physical behavior exhibited by systems with like properties.

Finally, a third family of related questions: What sequence of events and processes has contributed to the formation of the Grand Canyon? What occurred on the surface of the moon to form the craters and other features visible to us? What is the history of life forms on earth? Does the visible universe of dispersing galaxies have a discernible history? If so, what is the character and chronology of that history?

While these questions may seem somewhat more difficult than most of those cited earlier, these too are examples of questions that are open to investigation by the natural sciences. Questions like these fall into the broad category of questions concerning the *formative history* of the earth and its inhabitants, of other bodies in the solar system, and of the entire observable universe. On the basis of what has been discovered during the past century or two, we judge that these fascinating questions concerning the formative history of physical systems, including living systems, also lie within the domain of the natural sciences and are fruitful questions that merit careful scientific investigation.[3]

At the risk of oversimplification, we shall say that all (or certainly the vast majority) of the questions that lie within the domain of natural science can be comfortably placed within one of the three categories just introduced: the categories of *physical properties, physical behavior* and *formative history*.[4] Furthermore, we find it helpful to note that these three categories may be viewed as subdivisions of a larger category of classification: the *inherent intelligibility* of the physical universe. But that very formal term requires further clarification.

By experience and reflection, the human race has come to view the physical world as intelligible, that is, capable of being understood at least in part. The physical universe exhibits properties that are stable and measurable. And when we observe the behavior of physical systems, we discover universally applicable patterns of physical behavior. We are able to make sense out of individual phenomena because they fit into larger patterns—patterns which are empirically accessible and discernible by human investigators.

Furthermore, because the values of physical properties and the patterns of physical behavior are stable, we are able to recognize numerous features of the world around us as the products or consequences of earlier events and processes. We have discovered that even the formative history of the physical universe is intelligible.

But why do we add the qualifier *inherent* when we say that the domain of natural science is limited to the inherent intelligibility of the physical universe? The answer can be stated very straightforwardly. In essence, we must include the qualifier *inherent* because the physical universe—the object of investigation by the natural sciences—is *not* all there is. There is more to reality than the physical alone.

..

Along with the physical world, for example, there exist the "worlds" of abstract ideas and transcendent beings, of profound concepts such as beauty and truth, of human emotions such as love and fear, of moral principles for good and right, and of spiritual beings and their actions. As whole persons, scientists may employ elements from these nonmaterial "worlds" in their personal efforts to understand the meaning of the physical universe, but such elements are not themselves the object of natural science.

As an intellectual discipline, natural science is not isolated from or unrelated to human concerns for all that transcends the realm of physical phenomena, but nevertheless it self-consciously restricts itself to the physical universe as the object of its study. Natural science is the investigation of what can be known from within the physical world itself, without reference to anything that is nonphysical. It seeks to know the character of the component parts of the physical universe and their relationship to one another, but it sets aside the matter of the relationship of the physical world to any beings or realms of reality that transcend the physical world.

Questions concerning transcendent relationships lie outside of the domain of natural science. Science is unable, for example, to say anything about the relationship of the world to a divine Creator. Questions concerning the relationship of the universe to God must be directed elsewhere. The silence of natural science on such matters must be honored by both theists and nontheists. Both must resist the temptation to coerce science into warranting (in the sense of proving) their particular religious perspective.

Science is well equipped to deal with scientific questions regarding the inherent intelligibility of the physical world, and religion is well equipped to deal with the religious question of the relationship of this universe to a transcendent deity. Natural science and religion each deserve to have their unique domains respected by the other. Only when the integrity of each domain is respected can questions concerning their relationship and interaction be fruitfully explored.

Questions Lying outside the Domain of Natural Science

Because of the importance of this distinction between the domains of inherent intelligibility and transcendent relationship, let us cite a couple of examples of matters on which the natural sciences, because of their limited domain, must maintain respectful silence.

1. While natural science can fruitfully investigate the formation *of various structures within the physical world, it is incapable of dealing with the ultimate* origin *of the world's existence.*

Because of a great deal of misunderstanding concerning the word *origin,* this statement must be clarified. Very often, the word *origin* is used as a substitute for the word *formation.* When geologists, for example, speak of the origin of the Grand Canyon they are concerned with the succession of events and processes that make up the formative history of this magnificent geological structure. The uplift of continental land masses and the process of fluid erosion are examples of phenomena relevant to canyon formation.

Similarly, when astronomers speak about the origin and evolution of planets or stars or galaxies, their concern is with the processes by which these celestial objects developed their present form from earlier structures. Even when cosmologists speak about the origin of the entire expanding universe, they speak in terms of those processes by which the present state of affairs developed from earlier states. In the context of purely scientific inquiry, a discussion of origins must necessarily be restricted to a consideration of the *formation* of physical structures within the universe, the existence of which is taken for granted.

The question of ultimate *origin,* however, goes far beyond the matter of formative history. When we ask, What is the ultimate origin of the universe? we are asking, What is the source for the very existence of the universe? What agent causes *something* to exist in place of *nothing?* Furthermore, we are asking not merely about the *beginning* of existence, but about the existence of the universe at all times—past, present and future—even about the existence of time itself. The question concerning the source, or cause, or *origin*, of existence is just as much a question about right now as it is about any other moment in time.

This question of ultimate origin, however, lies well outside of the domain of natural science. We are able scientifically to deal with many kinds of events that happen in time, but we are unable to deal in the same way with questions concerning the source of time's very existence. We are not saying that the question concerning the origin of the universe cannot be asked; we are only saying that any consideration of its answer takes us beyond the domain of natural science and into the domain of philosophy (metaphysics) or religion.

A diversity of answers has been offered. According to philosophical naturalism, for example, the universe is self-originating, that is, its existence is independent of any nonphysical creative agent. In Christian theology, on the other hand, the origin of the world's existence is dependent at all times on the active will of God, the Creator—just as dependent at this moment as at any other moment, even the "beginning" of time.

Questions of *origin*—the ultimate source of existence itself—are profoundly important questions. Their answers, however, will never be derived from the results of natural science. They are religious questions that must be directed to whatever serves as the source of one's answers to religious questions. The natural sciences, because of limitations in both the object and the domain of their investigation, have no choice but to remain silent.

2. *While natural science can fruitfully investigate the* behavior *of the physical universe, it is incapable of settling the fundamental question concerning its* governance.

Just as *formation* and *origin* must be distinguished, so also *behavior* and *governance* must be distinguished—particularly in discussions concerning the relationship between science and religion. And, in a manner similar to our first distinction, we shall find one concept—*behavior*—to lie within the scientific domain and the other—*gover-*

nance—to lie outside of its boundary.

When natural scientists investigate the behavior of a physical system, they are concerned principally with the empirically accessible physical processes that take place within that system or with physical interactions between that system and its environment. Geologists, for example, are concerned with the behavior of the earth's crust in response to processes occurring within the earth itself and in response to earth's interactions with the sun and the moon. Chemists are concerned with the structure of atoms and with interactions among various atoms and molecules in a diversity of environmental conditions. Physicists seek to understand the behavior of physical systems and their interactions in terms of fundamental forces related to the physical properties of matter. And biologists endeavor to understand the physical behavior of living systems in terms of the structure and behavior of the cell and its constituent parts and in terms of the interaction of an organism with its environment. In each case, natural scientists are concerned to describe the observable behavior of some physical system and to discover the general patterns of behavior into which any specific phenomenon can be placed.

The search for a comprehensive set of interrelated patterns is the heart of the scientific enterprise. Our descriptions of these universal patterns of physical behavior are known by various generic titles: *scientific theories* or *theoretical models* or *laws of nature,* for instance. Specific examples include the special theory of relativity, the kinetic-molecular model for gases and the law of energy conservation. (We make no hard and fast distinction among the terms *theory, model* and *law;* these terms are nearly interchangeable, and the association of any one of them with a particular concept is more a matter of historical accident than of rigorous classification.)

To illustrate the behavior-governance distinction, let's take the law of energy conservation as an example. According to this "law," all physical systems behave in such a way that the total amount of energy possessed by the system and its environment remains constant.

Energy, we say, is always conserved; it can be neither created nor destroyed—only changed in form or transferred from one system to another. The law of energy conservation is a remarkably useful statement describing a very important aspect of the behavior of physical systems. Natural science, by empirically investigating the behavior of a wide variety of physical systems, has discovered a certain regular pattern to physical behavior and has formulated the law of energy conservation to describe that behavior pattern.

But why does the physical world behave in accordance with that pattern, or any other pattern? What power or agent *governs* physical behavior in a manner described by the energy conservation law? People sometimes speak as if the law itself governs that behavior; those introductory textbook discussions cited earlier are notorious for their talk about the "laws of nature that govern the behavior of physical systems."

Such talk, however is quite empty. The "laws of nature" are only our descriptions of the patterns of material behavior, and descriptions have no power to govern. The question of governance cannot be answered by describing patterns of behavior. Behavior patterns give evidence of a governing power at work, but such patterns are not themselves the source of governance. Behavior patterns are not the *cause* of governance; they are only the *result*.

Like the question of origin, the question of governance is fundamentally a religious question. Let's try to illustrate that by noting the difference between the answers provided by two very different religious perspectives that are prominent in Western culture: philosophical naturalism (or materialism), and Christian theism. According to naturalism, there exist no transcendent beings; the physical world is all there is. The governance of material behavior must be performed by matter itself. Matter, according to naturalism, is self-governing—autonomous.

Judeo-Christian theism, on the other hand, identifies God as the Governor of physical behavior. What we customarily call the "laws of

nature" are really our descriptions of the patterns of divine governance. These are not laws *of* nature for its self-governance, but rather
they are the intelligible manifestations of God's will *for* the behavior
of the created world. Physical behavior, according to theism, is not
autonomous (self-governed), but theonomous (God-governed).

In the light of this behavior-governance distinction, it should be
evident that the proponents of naturalism and of theism need have
no disagreements concerning the proper description for the patterns
of physical behavior. Provided that they do their scientific work in
conformity with the accepted standards for competence and integrity
and in the context of the community of professional natural scientists,
persons with vastly differing religious commitments can and do work
together toward the common goal of understanding the behavior of
the physical universe—the object of scientific investigation.

However, while theists and philosophical naturalists need not disagree on matters of physical *behavior,* they are in profound disagreement on the matter of *governance.* But the choice between an autonomous or a theonomous perspective on the governance of physical
behavior cannot be settled on the basis of scientific investigation. The
proponents of these two differing religious perspectives need not
work toward the development of different and competing scientific
descriptions of behavior, even though they seek to understand the
governance of that behavior within the frameworks of very different
religious perspectives. From the one perspective, matter is both self-
existent and self-governing; from the other, God is the ultimate reality
and the physical world is dependent on God for both its existence
(origin) and its governance.

Maintaining Proper Boundaries

Locating the boundary of the domain of natural science is of crucial
concern to those of us who wish to establish and maintain an ami-
cable working relationship between science and religion. The approach taken in this book is based on the recognition that while the

object of investigation by the natural sciences is the entire observable physical universe and its constituent parts—every physical thing that is empirically accessible—the *domain* of scientific inquiry is restricted to the inherent intelligibility of this universe. Working within this domain, natural scientists are capable of investigating the remarkable degree of intelligibility that is resident within the physical universe itself—in its physical properties, in its patterns of physical behavior and in its formative history.

On the other hand, questions concerning the relationship of the physical universe to any transcendent realm lie outside of the scientific domain. Such profound questions lie within the domain of religious or philosophical (metaphysical) inquiry. Consequently, while natural science can deal fruitfully with the formative history of the universe, questions concerning the origin, or source, of its existence must be directed elsewhere.

Similarly, while questions concerning physical behavior are appropriate questions for scientific inquiry, the question concerning the identity of the governing agent must be recognized as a religious question. Questions of origin and governance—important questions both—must be directed toward whatever serves as the source of answers to one's religious questions. And while the public-school classroom may be an appropriate place to raise these questions and to identify their religious significance, each student must seek answers within the context of his or her home community. On such matters the natural sciences have nothing to contribute.

THE PATH

MOST

TRAVELED

2

H AVING DISCUSSED BOTH THE OBJECT *AND THE domain* of the natural sciences, we now move on to consider the path followed by the scientific community as it seeks to achieve one of its principal *goals*. The scientific enterprise has many goals: to provide the means for controlling our environment; to provide the foundation for technology; to ensure our comfort, health and safety; and many others. Our present concern, however, is with natural science's goal of obtaining knowledge—sometimes referred to as its *epistemic* goal—its effort to gain knowledge about the physical properties, behavior and formative history of the world in which we live.

The principal forms of this knowledge are the results of empirical investigation and the products of scientific theorizing about the composition, structure, behavior and history of the physical systems that we observe. The empirical and theoretical components of this knowledge are closely interrelated and equally important. For this reason science education seeks both to train students to perform competent empirical investigation and to familiarize students with the array of scientific theories that contribute to the contemporary picture of the physical universe.

In this chapter we focus our attention on the system of *values* that functions in the process of scientific theorizing. While students of the natural sciences spend large amounts of time learning the *content* of numerous theories, and the developers of modern technology expend the majority of their effort in the creative and effective *application* of such theories, professional natural scientists direct their primary efforts toward the construction and *evaluation* of theories about physical phenomena.

Judging the merits of a particular scientific theory or choosing one theory from a set of competing theories concerning the same phenomena is a common activity within the scientific community. But on what basis are such judgments and choices made?

A half century ago it was commonly supposed that there existed some set of self-evident and rigidly applicable rules by which the truth or falsehood of a particular theory could be established once and for all. During the past few decades, however, historians and philosophers of science have developed a more realistic assessment of the way in which the scientific community functions.

It is now generally agreed that scientific theorizing is very little like the positivist* picture of the mechanical application of rigid logical *rules*, but is rather a *value*-guided activity of human judgment applied to the products of creative insight. Scientific theories cannot be con-

---

*Positivism is a philosophical perspective that rests on the assertion that authentic knowledge can be obtained only from "positive," that is, scientifically verifiable, information.

structed by a robotic assembly line, nor can theory evaluation be adequately performed by a roomful of even the most powerful of today's electronic computers.

If we wish to understand the process of scientific theory evaluation, we must see it as a wholly human enterprise. It is an activity performed by a community of persons—persons with finite knowledge, skills and insights—who must continually make judgments concerning the adequacy of scientific theories to account for the results of empirical investigation. Judgments must, of necessity, be based on accepted standards or values. On this system of values that the professional scientific community uses to evaluate theories we now focus our attention.

There exists no authoritative document which spells out the rules for scientific investigation, not even for the more restricted activity of theory evaluation. In the absence of such a canonical source the best we can do is to appeal to scientific practice itself in order to determine what general principles or value systems appear to operate. What follows, therefore, is a summary of insights into the historical practice of natural science provided by several observers of the scientific enterprise.[1] The list is by no means exhaustive. We shall limit ourselves to brief discussions of four categories of values—four categories of functioning criteria for judging the quality of scientific research or the adequacy of a scientific theory.[2]

Matters of Competence

Scientific research and theorizing is composed of a rich diversity of actions performed by scientists. For example, a long-range research program is planned, motivated by factors as varied as the colors in a rainbow; a specific question is posed for investigation; the investigators thoroughly familiarize themselves with the relevant literature; an empirical strategy is formulated; apparatus is selected or designed and assembled; the physical system or sample of material to be investigated is prepared; arrangements are made to control the environmental conditions; the measurement system is calibrated against an accepted standard; the degree of uncertainty in measured values is assessed; the observations or measurements of interest are performed and the relevant data are recorded; measurements may be repeated; the data are analyzed; the results are organized for presentation in the form of verbal descriptions, tables of numerical values, graphs, algebraic relationships, or the like; the results may be compared with predictions or expectations; inferences concerning relevant theories are drawn, or a new theory may be proposed to account for the empirical results; suggestions for further related research are offered, leading, perhaps, to a similar cycle of empirical and theoretical activity.

As a general rule, every one of these activities constituting scientific research requires a certain degree of familiarity with procedure and skill in performance. To be a good natural scientist, one *must* acquire the knowledge and the skills that are needed to perform these empirical, analytical and theoretical operations with competence. Such craft competence is highly valued within the professional scientific community. The tradition of high expectations for competent performance is passed on from one generation of scientists to the next. Incompetent work is universally rejected.

But surely this demand for competence comes as no surprise. The primary goal of natural science is authentic knowledge concerning the character of the physical universe. The only paths leading toward that goal are those paved with the results of competent performance of the empirical and theoretical crafts; good intentions are not enough. Incompetent performance in scientific investigation is the pavement of a one-way path to misperception, delusion and false conclusions—no friends of knowledge. But, of course, incompetent performance is unwelcomed in any field of endeavor.

Matters of Integrity
Scientific investigation is performed by a community of persons who, of necessity, must depend on the professional integrity of the other

members of that community. While research performed by one person or group may, for a variety of substantial reasons, be challenged and repeated by another, more commonly research reports are trusted to represent the results of competent work honestly reported. The *significance* of the report is open to question; the *convincing power* of its argumentation is subject to critical evaluation; but its *integrity* is expected to meet the unwritten, but nonetheless functional, code of professional ethics. Without a functioning set of ethical principles for integrity, the professional scientific community could not perform in the manner it presently does.

The fundamental principles are honesty, fairness and candor. Unquestionably, the willful propagation of reports that are known to be false or unreliable is totally unacceptable. And when observations or measurements are reported, we expect not only that the report provides an honest account of the results, but also that all reasonable precautions have been taken to ensure that these empirical results are reliable within limits that have been realistically assessed and candidly stated. If in the course of a computation one needs to use data obtained by other researchers, it is expected that the literature has been thoroughly searched in order to obtain the most reliable data available, often the data most recently reported. Unreliable, outdated or discredited reports should never knowingly be employed in support of one's case. Professional scientists are expected to exercise whatever level of diligence and self-discipline is required to minimize the propagation of false or misleading reports.

The process of extrapolation deserves special attention in the context of this discussion of professional integrity. Ordinarily the data base for the description of some behavior pattern is confined to a restricted range of circumstances. Any extrapolation of behavior patterns beyond those limits must be performed with appropriate restraint, and the conditions for the credibility of that extrapolation must be candidly stated.

If such restraint is not exercised with integrity, the results are likely to be meaningless at best and grossly misleading for those unprepared to assess the credibility of a given extrapolation. Mark Twain provides us with a very colorful example of the ridiculous conclusions that can be drawn from unrestrained extrapolation.

> In the space of one hundred and seventy-six years the Lower Mississippi has shortened itself two hundred and forty-two miles. This is an average of a trifle over one mile and a third per year. Therefore, any calm person, who is not blind or idiotic, can see that in the Old Oolithic Silurian Period, just a million years ago next November, the Lower Mississippi River was upward of one million three hundred thousand miles long, and stuck out over the Gulf of Mexico like a fishing-rod. . . . There is something fascinating about science. One gets such wholesale returns of conjecture out of such a trifling investment of fact. (from *Life on the Mississippi*, p. 155)

Professional scientists concur wholeheartedly with the thrust of Twain's conclusion: The offspring of unrestrained extrapolation is unmitigated nonsense.

Several matters of integrity are involved also in the manner in which one argues in favor of a particular theoretical model. We expect, for instance, that all relevant data will be given fair and adequate treatment—not only the supportive data but also the data which tell against the model. Anomalous or contradictory evidence may not be neglected or hidden. And if there are other phenomena or theories relevant to the one under evaluation, we expect the writer of the research report to bring such matters to the attention of the reader and to demonstrate how they strengthen or weaken the case.

This is particularly important when arguing in favor of a theory which makes strong claims for its superiority over a conventionally accepted alternative. Thus, in addition to the specific data and phenomena that are being investigated, the context of the investigation provided by other relevant data, phenomena and theories must be honestly engaged. Theorizing which, by conscious choice or by gross neglect, fails to pay due attention to this context also fails to meet the standards of professional integrity which are necessary for the proper functioning of the scientific community.

Matters of Sound Judgment

Suppose, now, that there are two or more competing theories which claim to account for relevant data and to provide the best explanation for a given phenomenon. When scientists encounter such situations, they are called on to judge the relative merits of competing theories and to make choices on the basis of certain criteria. Assuming that the criteria for competent research and honest analysis have already been satisfied, what additional criteria does the scientific community employ in its evaluation of competing theories? Following the suggestion of Professor Ernan McMullin (History and Philosophy of Science Program, University of Notre Dame), we shall refer to these as *epistemic values*—the criteria used to evaluate the scientific merit of a theory, that is, its likelihood of being authentic knowledge concerning the actual state of affairs.

Just as there is no standard list of professional ethical values, there is no standard list of epistemic values. No professional scientific organization has undertaken, nor is any likely to undertake, the formulation of a program for scoring or grading a theoretical model. That's not the way value judgments are made. However, for the purpose of illustrating how the scientific community does go about the business of theory appraisal, let's list examples of relevant epistemic values. McMullin cites six—predictive accuracy, internal coherence, external consistency, unifying power, fertility and simplicity.[3] Our list is a somewhat modified version of his.

1. Cognitive relevance. The supply of diverse theories concerning some aspect of the composition, structure, behavior or history of the physical realm appears to be inexhaustible. But many of these theories (especially those proposed by persons who are not specialists in the area under consideration) fail to be of any value to natural science because they fail to have cognitive relevance—that is, they fail seriously to engage the relevant empirical evidence.

For example, college science teachers often receive personal letters or copies of privately published papers which claim to present grand theories that "solve the great riddles of the universe" and so on, purportedly, will replace the whole array of conventional scientific theories. These proposals, usually written by persons with little scientific training, have as one of their characteristic features the absence of meaningful contact with specific empirical data relevant to the phenomena under discussion. References to actual physical properties or behavior will be very general and vague at best. Such proposals, because of their lack of engagement with actual data, are of no use in the search for knowledge. They may themselves provide the data for an interesting psychological study, but they contribute nothing to our understanding of the physical world.

In addition to such obviously deficient proposals, numerous other theories about the physical world, especially about its formative history, have been constructed with little or no regard for the actual physical data which are readily available in published literature. The impetus for these theories may be the desire to reinforce some philosophical or political perspective or to provide support for some religious concept.

The elements which comprise the theory or historical scenario may be drawn from sources or traditions considered to be relevant and authoritative by a particular ideological community, from imaginative speculation or from both. However, even when such theories are proposed by intelligent and sincere persons, even by educated scholars, they provide little or no assistance in achieving the epistemic goal of the natural sciences.

Any theory that fails to engage the relevant empirical data fails to be a theory about the world as it is. Any theory about cosmic history, for example, that neglects the storehouse of empirically derived knowledge about the world as observed can be no more than a theory about some hypothetical world, a make-believe world designed to conform to a set of preconceived requirements. Natural science, on the other hand, seeks knowledge concerning the world in which we actually live. Its theories, therefore, must fully engage the results of empirical investigation or be judged to have little value.

2. Predictive accuracy. As a general rule, an authentically scientific theory provides a means of predicting the values of measurable properties or the behavioral characteristics that a given physical system should exhibit. The obvious question to ask is, How well do the predicted quantities or behavior patterns compare with those observed? Thus, in assessing the merit of one or more theoretical models, the criterion of predictive accuracy is surely relevant.

A model which displays greater predictive accuracy than some competing model would ordinarily be favored. There is, however, no absolute guarantee that the model favored on the basis of this single criterion will in the long run prove to be the better one. Ptolemy's geocentric model for the solar system may have had greater predictive accuracy than the heliocentric model suggested earlier by Aristarchus, but we now know that the heliocentric model, as improved later by Copernicus, Kepler and Newton, has clearly demonstrated its superiority in a number of different ways, including predictive accuracy.

A slight variation on this criterion may be applied to the investigation of formative history. Our concern here is not to predict what will happen in the future, but rather to construct a plausible scenario for what happened in the past, thereby forming what we are now able to observe. The relevant question to ask of a formative-history model is, How well does that historical reconstruction account for the present state of affairs? Would the proposed formative history lead us to expect all of the features that have already been observed? Would the model also predict the presence of features not yet investigated? And when investigators look for these predicted features, are they found to be there? If so, one's confidence in the credibility of that formative-history scenario is legitimately increased.

3. Coherence. To persons who have grown up in the environment of twentieth-century Western culture, it is perhaps self-evident that an adequate scientific theory should be internally coherent, that it should contain no elements that are logically inconsistent with other elements. We assume that the behavior of physical systems is rationally intelligible, and consequently we expect that our theoretical models for their behavior will be devoid of any internal contradictions.

But the criterion of coherence has an even broader scope. We expect that not only will the behavior of a particular system or category of systems be internally coherent, but also that the physical behavior of the entire empirically accessible universe will be rationally coherent. Patterns of physical behavior are presumed to be universally applicable—the same patterns in all places and at all times and for all relevant systems.

The law of energy conservation, for instance, applies not only here on earth, but within the Andromeda Galaxy as well; not only today, but three billion years ago in the quasar 3C 273 as well; not only for falling apples, but for nuclear reactions as well.

In the context of such expectations, then, we would ordinarily judge that a scientific theory should display not only an internal coherence, but also a coherence with respect to the entire spectrum of physical phenomena and their associated theoretical models. The adequacy of any theory will, in part, be judged on the basis of its coherence relative to other theories already judged to have merit.

4. Explanatory scope. The scientific community does not rest comfortably with unexplained coincidence. To cite a classic example, the Ptolemaic geocentric model for the solar system left two specific features of the apparent motion of planets without explanation. The phenomenon of limited elongation (restricted angular distance from the sun) exhibited by Mercury and Venus required the Ptolemaic model to constrain the epicycle centers for these two planets to lie along the earth-sun line. Why should their motion satisfy this constraint? No explanation. Within the Ptolemaic model this constraint stood as an unexplained coincidence.

A similar appraisal applies to the observation that the fastest retrograde motion exhibited by Mars, Jupiter and Saturn always occurs when the planet is in opposition to the sun—another unexplained coincidence within the framework of Ptolemy's earth-centered geometry. In the sun-centered models of Copernicus and Kepler, however, both of these phenomena came to be recognized as natural consequences of the heliocentric geometry of the models. The explanatory scope, or inclusiveness, of the sun-centered models was greater than that of the Ptolemaic geocentric model. Unexplained coincidences were transformed into natural consequences.

Modern examples exist as well. For instance, the three-to-one dominance by mass of hydrogen over helium in the chemical composition of the physical universe is no longer considered to be a curious accident but rather the natural consequence of early cosmic history. The ability of the "standard model" in contemporary cosmology to explain this feature is considered to be a strong point in its favor. Theories with greater explanatory scope are generally judged to have greater epistemic merit.

5. Unifying power. The scientific community seeks not only to develop theories with sufficient explanatory scope to eliminate unexplained coincidences, it also seeks to unify what may once have been viewed as unrelated phenomena, each with their independent theories, into a single, more comprehensive theoretical framework. The effort by elementary particle theorists today to develop a single theory that will encompass the four (or will it be five?) fundamental forces provides a superb example of this goal. In the nineteenth century, James Clerk Maxwell successfully unified electrical and magnetic phenomena with his theory of electromagnetism. Today's theoretical physicists seek to develop yet another theory which will allow us to view the electromagnetic force, the weak nuclear force, the strong nuclear force and the gravitational force as but differing manifestations of a single "superforce."[4] It is remarkable how much progress toward this unification of forces has already been achieved.

But even on scales far less grand than that envisioned for "super-force" theory, those scientific theories which are able to unify diverse phenomena into one comprehensive theoretical framework will be favored over a collection of independent theories that treat each phenomenon in isolation from the others. The greater the unifying power of a theory, the better able it is, we judge, to demonstrate the inherent intelligibility of the physical world.

6. Fertility. The criterion, or epistemic value, of fertility is a bit more elusive than those already discussed. The five criteria cited above are concerned primarily with the question, How well does a given theory account for what we already know? Here, on the other hand, we are concerned to assess how well a theory functions to stimulate investigation in new areas, to suggest new ways of organizing our knowledge, to reveal relationships previously obscured, and the like. In each case the quality under scrutiny and assessment is the potency of a theory for stimulating the imagination and for initiating the propagation of a continuing line of helpful insights.

More epistemic values could be cited, though perhaps with diminished consensus among the philosophers and practitioners of science concerning their importance within the scientific enterprise. Among those already cited there is unavoidably some overlap. Furthermore, though we have chosen to arrange our list in a particular order, we make no claim that this represents the order of their functional importance.

With McMullin, we intend here only to call attention to the idea that theory assessment and theory choice in natural science is not principally a matter of mechanically scoring a theory according to some fixed set of self-evident rules, nor merely a matter of expressing one's personal opinion, but rather more like the process of making value judgments, something everyone does every day. These judgments are based on the system of *epistemic values* found within the scientific community—values inherited from previous generations, modeled by senior members of the community, strengthened or modified by experience, applied in varying ways by members of the community, and permitting a healthy level of disagreement within the context provided by a broad foundation of consensus.

Extra-Scientific Matters

We have called attention to numerous constraints on the scientific enterprise that have evolved within the community of practicing scientists. The object of scientific investigation is not all of reality, only the physical world. The domain of natural science does not encompass all categories of questions about the physical world, only those questions concerning its inherent intelligibility. Operating within the boundaries of that domain, members of the scientific community are further constrained by their professional colleagues to meet the community's standards for craft competence, to carry out and report their research with ethical integrity, and to evaluate scientific theories on the basis of a communally developed epistemic value system.

But what, we now ask, do scientists do with their concepts and beliefs concerning the rest of reality? Must their scientific work be completely isolated from their concerns in the arenas of religion, philosophy, politics, economics, social institutions, personal ambitions and the arts? Won't these cultural, ideological, personal, religious and other extra-scientific concerns—concerns for matters outside of the scientific domain—have a discernible influence on one's scientific work? If so, what is the character and extent of this influence?

Identifying the roles played by extra-scientific concerns in the scientific enterprise is a complex and difficult task. It is an area of study that deserves continuing attention. For our present purposes we shall focus briefly on the function of religious commitments in scientific investigation. The term *religious commitment* must not be interpreted too narrowly, however. We do not wish, for instance, to restrict it to the Christian religion, not even to theism in general. Rather, we intend the term to represent the full spectrum of beliefs concerning the ultimate nature of reality, the existence or nonexistence of a transcendent deity, the significance of human life, and the relationship of the physical world to any transcendent beings or realms of reality. Thus twentieth-century Western naturalism is as much a religious commitment as is Christian theism.

First, religious commitments frequently serve as a stimulus for a scientist to select and carry out a particular program of research. Certain topics for investigation may be given priority because of their relevance to an investigator's world view—his or her "vision of reality." We see no reason to criticize or discourage this kind of influence. On the contrary, it would appear to be a wholly appropriate way to act with integrity in the context of one's religious commitments.

Second, religious commitments ought never lead a scientist to permit or encourage any reduction in the demands for craft competence or professional integrity. In order for the epistemic goal of natural science—the gaining of knowledge—to be achieved, each member of the community must honor the requirements for competence and integrity and must participate in the process of mutual discipline which functions to maintain those standards.

Third, religious commitments cannot be used as a warrant to ignore or to consciously violate the boundaries of the scientific domain. While the domain of one's personal concerns will inevitably extend beyond the boundaries of natural science, no scientist has the right to claim that natural science itself has the ability or authority to settle issues outside of the domain of inherent intelligibility that we described earlier.

For example, the oft-heard claims that natural science either confirms or discredits a theistic concept of divine governance or validates some particular concept of the status of the physical universe in relationship to deity is careless talk that exposes a failure to honor the boundaries of the scientific domain. Such a mischievous violation of domain boundaries is likely to be damaging to the credibility of authentic scientific results and, in the long run, will do a particular religious perspective no favor. Linking a specific scientific model to some religious belief system, for example, has the strategic disadvantage that a discrediting of that scientific model automatically calls into question the entire belief system attached to it. Alliances of religious belief and scientific theory should be formed only with great care and restraint.

Fourth, religious commitments, whether theistic or nontheistic, should not be permitted to interfere with the normal functioning of the epistemic value system employed within the scientific community. Great mischief is done when extra-scientific dogma is allowed to substitute for epistemic values such as cognitive relevance, predictive accuracy, coherence, explanatory scope, unifying power and fertility. And progress toward the goal of authentic knowledge is likely to be impeded when religious commitment is permitted to so skew the theory-evaluation process that one epistemic value takes inordinate precedence over all others.

The troublesome tendency with which we are dealing here is the temptation to employ natural science for the purpose of supporting preconceptions drawn from one's philosophical commitments or system of religious beliefs. But such an approach stands the scientific enterprise on its head and must be resolutely avoided. The goal of natural science is to gain knowledge, not to reinforce preconceptions. The purpose of empirical research is to discover what the physical world is really like, not to verify its conformity to our preferences. And the aim of scientific theorizing is to describe the actual character of the universe, not to force its compliance with our preconceived requirements

Science held hostage by any ideology or belief system, whether naturalistic or theistic, can no longer function effectively to gain knowledge of the physical universe. When the epistemic goal of gaining knowledge is replaced by the dogmatic goal of providing warrant for one's personal belief system or for some sectarian creed, the superficial activity that remains may no longer be called natural science.

It may be termed *world-view warranting* or *creed confirmation,* or one may put it into the category of *folk science,*[5] but it no longer deserves the label of *natural science* because it is no longer capable of giving birth to knowledge. Science held hostage by extra-scientific dogma is science made barren.

Are we then left with the implication that religious belief is held hostage by the results of an autonomous natural science? Emphatically not! Recall from our earlier discussion that science and religion have differing domains of concern. Consequently, each needs to learn from the other concerning what lies outside of its own domain. And those of us who wish to build a comprehensive world view must learn from both so that we may come to know not only the inherent intelligibility of the physical universe, but also its place in the whole of reality.

The scientific community seeks to gain knowledge in a manner that honors the religious diversity of its membership. When speaking on matters concerning the ultimate significance of the composition, structure or formative history of the universe, individual scientists may disagree sharply because of their differing religious commitments. However, when working within the restricted domain of natural science, scientists are able to function as a community united in the search for authentic knowledge concerning the inherent intelligibility of the physical world. The results of professional natural science belong to everyone; any attempt to declare them the exclusive property of one specific religious perspective must be rejected.

A question of direct concern to many Christians is, Does the Bible provide any data relevant to the construction or evaluation of theories in the natural sciences? Persons equally committed to the Christian faith differ widely in their judgment in this matter.[6] Some persons, for example, judge that the Bible provides data relevant to theories concerning the events, processes and chronology of the formative history of the universe. Others are convinced that it was never intended to address such concerns.

Resolution of these differences is not a simple matter. The Bible contains a rich diversity of forms of historical literature—forms often very different from what we are accustomed to. Furthermore, the agenda of the Bible's historical literature is authentic to its ancient Near Eastern cultural and religious context—a setting quite different from our modern Western world. Thus all persons, whether committed to the Christian faith or not, must exercise great care and caution in making statements about biblical data and its relevance to contemporary scientific theorizing.

SCIENCE
HELD HOSTAGE
BY CREATIONISM
PART II

Having described the principal criteria for evaluating the adequacy of scientific theories, we will in the remainder of this book offer several case studies which illustrate what happens when this value system is violated. Our special concern in this section is to document how a commitment to the "scientific creationist" picture of cosmic history has functioned to diminish the demand for both craft competence and professional integrity and to disable the generally accepted epistemic value system. When natural science is held hostage to support preconceived answers, it can no longer serve in the open-minded search for knowledge.

THE LEGEND

OF THE

SHRINKING SUN

3

I
N JUNE 1979 A PAPER ENTITLED "SECULAR DECREASE
in the Solar Diameter, 1836-1953" was presented at a meeting of the American Astronomical Society.[1] In this report
John Eddy, a respected solar astronomer, and his col-
league Aram Boornazian presented an analysis of solar
meridian transit records from the Royal Greenwich Observatory—
records from which they computed the time required for the sun to
cross the celestial meridian at noon. Their analysis of this data suggested that during the specified time period the sun's angular diameter had been contracting at a rate of more than two arc seconds per
century, equivalent to a linear shrinkage rate of five feet per hour.

Figure 1 shows how the Greenwich data encourage such a conclusion. Furthermore, the case for solar shrinkage over an extended time

period appeared to be strengthened by an appeal to a 1567 report of a solar eclipse which suggested that the eclipse was annular rather than total.[2] If the sun had been the same size then as now, a total eclipse should have been observed.

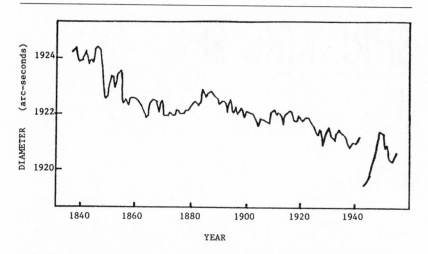

Figure 1. The horizontal (east-west) diameter of the sun from 1836 to 1953 as determined by Eddy and Boornazian from the Royal Greenwich Observatory data. (This figure is adapted from the diagram published in *Physics Today*, ref. 2.)

Eddy and Boornazian's report generated considerable interest because it presented the astronomical community with a puzzle: If the sun has behaved in the manner suggested by that report, then the sun has been far more variable than paleoclimatic evidence and conventional solar models have led us to believe. The combination of extended duration and high rate of variation in the sun's diameter was especially puzzling.

Rapid changes of short duration can be understood in terms of numerous transient and oscillatory phenomena. Relatively slow change, either contraction or expansion, extending over a period of hundreds or even thousands of years could also be the consequence of oscillatory or temporary changes in the behavior of the solar interior.[3] But a truly secular shrinkage—that is, a steady decrease in size over an indefinitely long period of time—would be at odds with contemporary models of solar behavior and inconsistent with geological evidence.

Prior to the discovery of the process of thermonuclear fusion, gradual gravitational contraction (commonly called "Helmholtz contraction") appeared to be the most likely candidate for the energy generating process in stars, including the sun. Since the 1930s, however, astrophysicists have become convinced that the thermonuclear-fusion process is responsible for maintaining stellar luminosity. According to contemporary stellar models, the physical conditions that prevail within the core of a star make the fusion process inevitable. As a consequence of changes brought about by thermonuclear fusion, a slow secular increase in stellar size is predicted—far too slow to observe with present instrumentation, but a secular *increase* nonetheless.

In the context of this prediction, Eddy and Boornazian's suggestion of a rapid secular *decrease* in solar diameter was especially intriguing. Even the *rate* of decrease was difficult to understand. Because a shrinkage rate of five feet per hour is hundreds of times greater than Helmholtz contraction could sustain, Eddy proposed that only the outermost, low-density portion of the sun was involved in contraction. In this way the rate of gravitational energy conversion into heat could still be lower than the sun's luminosity value. Even with this interpretation, however, Eddy and Boornazian's report was provocative, and it stimulated a heightened interest in both the rate and duration of variations in the sun's size.

The rate of solar shrinkage suggested by Eddy and Boornazian was disputed from the outset. In the same month that Eddy and Boornazian's preliminary report was presented, S. Sofia, J. O'Keefe, J. R. Lesh and A. S. Endal published an article in *Science* that expressed the judgment that, on the basis of available data (mostly from meridian transit observations), the sun's angular diameter did not diminish by more than 0.5 arc second between 1850 and 1937.[4] This value was less than one-fourth the rate proposed by Eddy and Boornazian.

In addition to the timing of solar meridian transits, other observations can be employed to determine the sun's diameter. In 1980 Irwin Shapiro published his analysis of the transits of Mercury in front of the sun from 1736 to 1973.[5] Shapiro concluded that no significant change in the sun's diameter could be detected and that the maximum shrinkage rate allowed by the data was 0.3 arc second per century, about one-seventh of the Eddy and Boornazian value. Figure 2 illustrates how the Mercury transit data contradict the Eddy and Boornazian proposal. Similarly, D. W. Dunham and others analyzed solar eclipse data and concluded that between 1715 and 1979 the sun's diameter may have decreased, but only by 0.7 arc second, equivalent to a rate of about 0.25 arc second per century.[6]

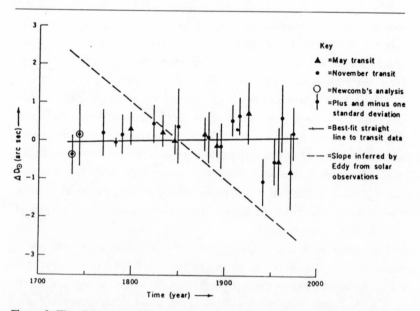

Figure 2. The diameter of the sun from 1723 to 1973 as computed by Irwin Shapiro from Mercury transit data. The dashed line represents the Eddy and Boornazian rapid shrinkage rate. (Diagram taken from ref. 5.)

The discrepancy between these results and the report by Eddy and Boornazian called for a second look at the solar meridian transit data. John H. Parkinson, Leslie V. Morrison and F. Richard Stephenson performed such a re-evaluation and concluded that the trends in the Greenwich data reported by Eddy and Boornazian "are the result of instrumental and observational defects rather than real changes."[7] In their judgment, based on the combined data sets of the Mercury transit and total solar eclipse observations, no secular change over the past 250 years was detectable, but a cyclic change with an 80-year periodicity was indicated. In an extensive article published in the *Astrophysical Journal*, R. L. Gilliland confirmed the presence of a 76-year periodic variation in the sun's diameter, but suggested that the data do allow for a very slow, long-term shrinkage at the rate of 0.1 arc second per century during the past 265 years.[8]

During the past few years, additional papers have been published which reinforce the conclusion that secular changes in solar diameter cannot be confirmed by available data, but numerous oscillatory phenomena have been verified. Parkinson, for example, in a 1983 paper, states that solar eclipse and Mercury transit measurements "confirm that there is no evidence for any secular changes in the solar diameter, with a reduced upper limit. However, there is increased support for an (approximately) 80-year cyclic variation."[9] And according to Sofia and others, "Solar radius changes are not secular (monotonic and uniform)."[10]

In 1984, Claus Frohlich and John Eddy reported the results of recent measurements of solar diameter.[11] Particularly relevant is their finding that, during the period from 1967-80, the sun exhibited an *increase* in diameter at the mean rate of 0.03 arc second per year, equivalent to a linear rate of eight feet per hour. Since 1980 the solar diameter has remained nearly constant, with a weak suggestion of decreasing. This behavior is remarkably consistent with the 76-year periodic behavior found by Parkinson and Gilliland, for which a broad maximum would be expected in the mid-1980s.

Where did Eddy and Boornazian go wrong? It appears that the Greenwich data contain some systematic errors which limit their reliability. As noted by Parkinson and others (see ref. 7) there were significant changes in both the method and the instrumentation employed in obtaining the Greenwich data. A number of discontinuities in the data can be correlated with these changes. Such phenomena, along with significant variations in both the skill of observers and the quality of observing conditions, place severe limitations on the reliability of some of the Greenwich data and on the credibility of the Eddy and Boornazian proposal concerning rapid solar shrinkage. The data on which Eddy and Boornazian based their conclusions are plagued with subtle flaws.

Reflections on the Professional Approach
This brief sketch of approximately six years of investigation regarding solar-size variations has concentrated on observational matters; we have not dealt extensively with theories concerning the physical processes which might generate these variations. Furthermore, we have been most concerned with secular (that is, long-term) variations, and have chosen not to discuss a number of short-term oscillations and fluctuations. In spite of these limitations, however, what we have considered here does provide us with an illustrative case study of the way in which professional natural science is performed. Let us highlight some of the characteristic features of this episode.

The question of solar-size variations is interesting mostly for its relevance to other phenomena. The temporal development of the sun's radius is an integral part of any theoretical model for solar behavior. Episodes of gravitational contraction, for instance, might be relevant to the resolution of the neutrino puzzle (to be discussed later in this chapter). And scientists who are interested in the history of the terrestrial climate are concerned to investigate the relationship of variations in solar radius to variations in the rate at which earth receives solar energy.

Eddy and Boornazian chose to look for variations in solar diameter by investigating historical records of solar meridian transits (that is, the rate at which the sun crosses a meridian). Their preliminary results suggested a long-term contraction at a surprisingly high rate. Though they did not consider their results ready for formal publication Eddy and Boornazian decided to present their puzzle in a brief talk at a meeting of the American Astronomical Society. In this way the professional scientific community could join them in a critical evaluation of the data and their interpretation.

The response of the scientific community was precisely as one should expect. Various investigators began to consider other relevant phenomena which might shed light on the puzzle. Data from solar eclipse observations and transits of Mercury, for example, were employed to generate independent computations of variations in solar diameter. The reliability of the meridian transit data was carefully scrutinized. And the results of these several investigations were published for further community evaluation.

By now the puzzle has largely been solved. The possibility of long-term, rapid shrinkage is *not* supported by the data. On the question of secular contraction or expansion at a very slow rate, the data are inconclusive. The limited precision of the data and the limited duration of the historical record preclude the employment of these data as the basis for any conjecture concerning the sun's size before about 1700. Any extrapolation of transit or eclipse data beyond three or four centuries is entirely unwarranted. Geological evidence for terrestrial climate variation provides a far more reliable indicator of solar dimensions prior to 1700.

All of the variation in solar diameter that is revealed by the transit and eclipse data can be identified with oscillatory and transient effects. The 80-year oscillation confirmed by this data had been anticipated on the basis of clues drawn from sunspot cycles. Although the investigations discussed in this chapter have not resolved the neutrino puzzle, neither do they offer any substantial encouragement for doubting that thermonuclear fusion is responsible for energy production in the sun. In fact, paleoclimatic evidence clearly discourages such a conjecture. And because of the strong influence of solar history on terrestrial history, conjectures concerning the history of solar behavior should never be made in isolation from a consideration of the physical record of terrestrial history.

From Puzzle to Proof: The Creation of a Legend

The puzzling report that there was evidence to suggest a rapid shrinkage of the sun over several centuries was quickly adapted by the creation-science community for use as a "scientific evidence," or "proof," for a very young earth. Without the extended duration of cosmic history, the concept of cosmic evolution would appear to be untenable. And, according to the proponents of creation-science, if evolution over a multibillion-year period did not take place, then creation (restricted to acts of inception) must have occurred during a very busy week about 10,000 years ago. Let us explore how the shrinking sun report has been employed as evidence in support of the young-earth hypothesis.

The basic framework was set in place by Russell Akridge. The Institute for Creation Research publishes a monthly series of brief, popular-level "vital articles on science/creation" under the heading of *Impact.* The April 1980 issue, entitled "The Sun Is Shrinking," was written by Akridge, a physicist at Oral Roberts University. Two elements characterize his approach: (1) an unquestioning acceptance of the solar shrinkage rate proposed by Eddy and Boornazian in 1979; and (2) an unrestrained extrapolation of that behavior into the indefinite past. Employing this approach, Akridge calculated that 100,000 years ago the sun would have been twice its present size, and that 20 million years ago it would have been as large as the earth's orbit, thereby precluding a multibillion-year duration for cosmic history and discrediting all concepts of evolution.

According to Akridge, not only did the shrinking sun phenomenon cast doubt on the standard chronology for terrestrial history, but it also had the potential for destroying the credibility of conventional astrophysical models for stellar behavior, ultimately dismantling the very concept of stellar evolution. By assuming that gravitational contraction had been amply demonstrated, Akridge concluded that the identification of thermonuclear fusion as the solar energy source was seriously threatened. In his words:

> The discovery that the sun is shrinking may prove to be the downfall of the accepted theory of solar evolution. . . . The entire theoretical description of the evolution of the universe may be at stake. . . . The changes detected in the sun call into question the accepted thermonuclear fusion energy source for the sun. This, in turn, questions the entire theoretical structure upon which the evolutionary theory of astrophysics is built.[12]

These were bold claims, asserting the imminent collapse of a major portion of the contemporary paradigm of astrophysics. The credibility of a scientific claim, however, is established not by its boldness, but by its adequacy to account for physical phenomena in an accurate, coherent and fruitful manner. How well did Akridge's claims hold up under the ordinary tests for scientific adequacy?

In order to support his assertions, Akridge needed to establish at least these two points: (1) that solar contraction over a period of a century or more was convincingly demonstrated by the empirical evidence; (2) that a contraction in the sun's diameter, if observed during a period of a few centuries, may be extrapolated indefinitely into the past. On the first point, Akridge was already on shaky ground. Recall that the 1979 paper published by Sofia and others placed a much lower limit on the rate of any possible shrinkage. Furthermore, the results of investigation concerning related phenomena, such as Mercury transits or solar eclipse observations, had not yet been published. Thus to speak of the Eddy and Boornazian result (published only as an abstract) as if it had convincingly established the occurrence of long-term solar shrinkage constituted a failure to exercise appropriate restraint in employing the results of a single investigation.

Though it may not have been apparent to his untrained readers, Akridge's uncritical acceptance of a single report—a report greeted with skepticism by the relevant professional community, a preliminary report not yet tested by comparison with other relevant studies— represented a serious failure to perform with integrity the critical evaluation expected of professional scientists.

The second failure is considerably more obvious. Not only did Akridge unquestioningly accept the Eddy and Boornazian preliminary result as if it had firmly established solar shrinkage, he extrapolated that behavior indefinitely into the remote past. Assuming, without sufficient warrant, a constant shrinkage rate, Akridge led the reader to believe that, had the sun existed 20 million years ago, it would necessarily have been as large as the earth's orbit. In performing such an extended extrapolation, Akridge chose to ignore the possibility of numerous transient and oscillatory phenomena with characteristic time periods as long as thousands of years.

As we indicated earlier in this discussion, any extrapolation of solar diameter variations beyond a few centuries would be entirely unwarranted, thereby representing unacceptable scientific practice. To base, as did Akridge, a bold and substantial claim on such an unwarranted extrapolation represents a serious failure to follow the fundamental principles for competent scientific investigation. And not only did Akridge presume the validity of this extrapolation, he even argued that to assume a constant shrinkage rate over extended time periods was a *conservative* assumption.

In spite of these and other shortcomings, however, the shrinking sun report, presented in the manner established by Akridge, continues to be employed as a "scientific evidence" for a young earth. In a 1982 article in *Christianity Today*, Thomas Barnes, then Dean of the Graduate School at the Institute for Creation Research, presented a list of six "evidences" for a recent creation.[13] Barnes concluded his list with an appeal to the shrinking sun report.

Though this was written three years after the Eddy and Boornazian report, Barnes gave no evidence of having taken into account the several professional publications which had cast serious doubt on the reality of secular solar shrinkage. Instead, Barnes simply repeated the Akridge analysis. In a handbook written to accompany the *ORIGINS* film series, distributed by Films For Christ, we also find the shrinking sun cited as evidence for a young earth.[14] The brief discussion follows the Akridge approach very closely; it even borrows from the *Impact* article a diagram which shows the earth skimming the surface of a bloated sun, presumably 20 million years ago.

Having lost contact with the results of continuing investigation and evaluation by the professional scientific community, the employment of the shrinking sun as an "evidence" for recent creation ceased to be authentically scientific. Instead, it took on the status of a legendary tale, recited to provide its hearers with the comforting reassurance that their recent-creation scenario was supported by empirical evidence.

Functioning to provide young-earth advocates with reassurance for their particular picture of God's creative activity, lists of "scientific evidences" serve as specimens of a creationist folk science.[15] One of the most lengthy of these lists can be found in the June, July and August 1984 issues of the *Bible-Science Newsletter*. Under the heading of "The Scientific Case for Creation," we find a list of 116 categories of evidence prepared by Dr. Walter T. Brown, Jr., a mechanical engineer. Number 85 on this list is the shrinking sun phenomenon. Brown's analysis is essentially the same as Akridge's. He treated secular contraction as if convincingly established and extrapolated that behavior indefinitely, on which basis he concluded that "had the sun existed a million years ago, it would have been so large that it would have heated the earth so much that life could not have survived."[16]

Henry Morris, President of the Institute for Creation Research, did no better than Akridge, Barnes or Brown. In his 1984 treatise on *The Biblical Basis for Modern Science*, Morris presented his vision of biblical insights into a broad spectrum of natural sciences. In a brief discussion on solar energy generation, Morris sought to argue that gravitational collapse, not thermonuclear fusion, is responsible for solar luminosity. The shrinking sun report was employed to bolster that argument:

> As a matter of fact, careful measurements in recent years have supported the collapse theory by showing that the sun's diameter does, indeed, appear to be shrinking. But this in turn would mean that the sun could not possibly be billions of years old![17]

This statement, made five years after Eddy and Boornazian's preliminary report, demonstrated no attempt to incorporate the results of the numerous, relevant investigations performed and reported during that five-year interval. Instead, Henry Morris, clearly the most influential person in the creation-science movement, propagated the same misrepresentation of solar behavior initiated by Akridge's 1980 *Impact* article.

The Shrinking Sun in the *Creation Research Society Quarterly*

Thus far the creation-science literature cited has been popular-level material intended for a general audience. Is it possible that the more technical literature of the recent-creationist community has done a better job of displaying a respect for the professional standards of the scientific community? As a general rule it has not, though there are exceptions.

For example, we should expect the *Creation Research Society Quarterly* to demonstrate a higher level of methodological competence and professional integrity. How have they handled the shrinking sun report? In a series of two articles, published in June and December of 1980, Hilton Hinderliter presented his analysis of this phenomenon.[18] Although these articles are anecdotal in style, very different from professional journal literature, we will assume that they were intended to be read as authentic specimens of creation-science, that is, informative analytical reports written by scientifically trained persons. (Dr.

Hinderliter is an assistant professor of physics at the New Kensington campus of Pennsylvania State University.) The scientific adequacy of the analysis, however, differs little from the popular material reviewed above.

Like Akridge, Hinderliter uncritically accepted the rapid shrinkage rate first reported by Eddy and Boornazian; he even praised the reliability of the historical data used by Eddy and the thoroughness of his data analysis. On the other hand, the judgment expressed by Eddy and many others[19] that the suspected variation was most likely a cyclic phenomenon was summarily dismissed as no more than the product of an unwarranted belief in what Hinderliter called the "billion year myth."

We find in this discussion no evidence of any careful evaluation of the merits of several suggested mechanisms that could introduce periodic variations in solar size.[20] Instead, the suggestion of periodic behavior was rejected as merely a product of an evolutionistic bias. Similarly, Hinderliter's ready acceptance of the conclusion drawn from one analysis of meridian transit data alone failed to recognize the relevance of data drawn from other phenomena, such as solar eclipse records, Mercury transit observations and the paleoclimatic record. None of these data were critically evaluated by Hinderliter; they were simply ignored or rejected as unworthy of consideration.

In his discussion of gravitational contraction as a possible source of solar energy, Hinderliter claimed that this mechanism had been rejected by the scientific community "solely on the basis of a supposed age of the earth in billions of years."[21] Furthermore, "the compelling force for the acceptance of vast ages was merely a faith in evolutionism, which itself has no evidential leg to stand on."[22] In summary, "evolutionism demanded a vast age for the sun, which in turn caused gravitational contraction to be ruled out as a major source of the sun's energy."[23]

A careful review of the relevant history, however, yields a significantly different conclusion. Because both geological and radiometric evidence indicated a terrestrial age of billions of years, the gravitational collapse lifetime for the sun—a few tens of millions of years—presented a real puzzle. When the process of thermonuclear fusion first became known, it was indeed greeted as a candidate for solar energy generation. But the transformation from candidate to accepted phenomenon could take place only with the development of a model for the sun which complied with all of the known patterns for material behavior and which would make fusion inevitable. Such has been the case.[24]

Nonetheless, by assuming that the meridian transit data had convincingly established a secular gravitational contraction of the sun and appealing to the surprisingly low solar neutrino flux as supporting evidence, Hinderliter concluded that the thermonuclear fusion model for solar energy production had been thoroughly discredited. In a manner very much like that of Russell Akridge, Hinderliter asserted that from his analysis of the shrinking sun report, "It is clear that we have witnessed a major scientific defeat for evolutionism."[25]

Although the papers by Hinderliter may fail to display the appropriate level of critical evaluation of the relevant phenomena, data and theoretical models, another paper, "The Sun's Luminosity and Age," written by James Hanson, suffers from even greater shortcomings. Hanson strongly favored a shrinking sun, such as reported by Eddy and Boornazian. The first reason cited by Hanson for this opinion was that "it is anti-evolutionary and compatible with the creationist view of a recently created, not evolved, sun."[26] He cited papers by Shapiro, Sofia and others,[27] but failed to deal substantively with their content. Their objections to Eddy and Boornazian's conclusions were categorically dismissed as the product of evolutionistic bias.

But the most bewildering component of Hanson's paper is his proposal of an "incandescence theory" for solar luminosity. He proposed that the sun was created 6000 years ago with a *uniform* temperature, and that it has been *uniformly* cooling off since that time. Solar luminosity, according to Hanson's model, derives simply from the thermal energy stored in the recently created sun. After performing some calculations which purport to show that the decrease in solar temperature during the past 6000 years would be acceptably small, Hanson says:

> Note that by this analysis we may infer that if the sun or a star were created isothermal it would stay nearly that way, which is, also, in direct contradiction to evolutionary astrophysics.[28]

Within the statement just quoted, we encounter at least three serious problems with Hanson's approach. First, the idea that the sun would, if created isothermal, remain isothermal cannot be *inferred* from Hanson's model; rather, it is no more than the unwarranted *assumption* on which the model is built.

Second, Hanson offered no demonstration that an isothermal solar model which complies with all relevant physical laws (concerning gravity, hydrostatic equilibrium, equation of state, etc.) can be constructed. In fact, the necessity of such a demonstration was not even recognized.

Third, and especially devastating, Hanson's incandescence model with its isothermal sun is in contradiction not only to "evolutionary astrophysics," it also stands in contradiction to a basic thermodynamic principle taught in most first-year general physics courses! Heat does not flow through an ordinary medium unless there is a temperature gradient. Hanson's isothermal sun would demand an infinite thermal conductivity (or some other means of unimpeded heat transfer) in order to remain at a uniform temperature while radiating energy from its surface. Contemporary models for the solar interior, on the other hand, indicate that a central temperature of greater than 10,000,000 degrees Kelvin is required to maintain an adequate heat flow from the core to the solar surface. The incandescence model proposed in Hanson's paper is wholly unrealistic.

Elsewhere in the paper, Hanson expressed a certain fondness for reviving theories from the past. In his closing statements Hanson favorably associated his incandescence model with pre-Copernican astronomy with these words:

> The incandescence theory would probably have been the explanation in pre-Copernican times. This is another example of the frequent superiority of pre-Copernican astronomy over the present Copernican-evolutionary views.[29]

An article of considerably higher quality, "Solar Neutrinos and a Young Sun," by Paul Steidl, can be found in the June 1980 issue of the *Quarterly*. Compared with the material written by Akridge, Hinderliter or Hanson, Steidl's paper demonstrated a far greater knowledge of astrophysics and a creditable awareness of relevant data and phenomena. The chief topic of the paper is the solar neutrino puzzle. Contemporary solar models predict the types and rates of thermonuclear fusion reactions that would occur in the sun, provided that our understanding of the relevant physical conditions and processes is adequate. During the past several years, measurements have been performed to determine the rate at which neutrinos, a byproduct of these fusion reactions, are being received on earth. The puzzling result is that the measured rate is only one-third of the expected rate.

Steidl's solution to this puzzle was to propose that no fusion whatsoever is occurring in the sun and that solar luminosity is derived solely from gravitational contraction, thereby discrediting any multibillion-year chronology for solar system history. In Steidl's words, "Thus the near absence of solar neutrinos alone is enough to indicate that the sun is considerably younger than usually assumed. . . . The sun is surely younger than its accepted (uniformitarian) age."[30]

In our judgment, however, Steidl paid far too little attention to a vast array of empirical and theoretical considerations which have led the professional scientific community to the well-founded *conclusion* (not assumption) that the solar system formed about 4.6 billion years ago. We suspect that it was Steidl's commitment to a recent-creation scenario, rather than a critical evaluation of the data, which played the decisive role in leading him to his conclusion. Yet Steidl himself accused the entire professional scientific community of a bias in favor of an ancient, evolved sun. "It [fusion] has become accepted dogma simply because it is the only conceivable process which could provide energy for the billions of years which stars are believed to have existed."[31]

Steidl offered a brief discussion of the solar shrinkage phenomenon as reported by Eddy and Boornazian. For Steidl this report was taken as confirmation that fusion is not occurring in the sun and that solar luminosity is powered by Helmholtz contraction. Regarding Eddy and Boornazian's own judgment that the solar shrinkage they reported was part of a cyclic phenomenon, Steidl said, "Of course they do not allow the possibility that it has been going on for more than a few hundred years, since this would totally dethrone stellar evolution."[32] By suppressing arguments based on the coherence of numerous empirical and theoretical considerations which have led scientists to their conclusions concerning an old and fusion-powered sun, claiming instead that these concepts are based *solely* on some form of evolutionistic bias, Steidl joined in the approach followed by Akridge, Hinderliter and Hanson.

But our review of Steidl's work can end on a much more positive note. In a brief letter published in the March 1982 *Quarterly*, Steidl alerted his readers to two significant developments.[33] First, the possibility of a nonzero rest mass for the neutrino would reduce the expected neutrino detection rate by a factor of three, consonant with the observed value. Steidl aptly concluded: "Perhaps the sun is burning hydrogen after all"—that is, converting hydrogen into helium through thermonuclear fusion. Second, Steidl called attention to several recently published papers which contest the reality of secular solar shrinkage. In advising his readers to suspend judgment on his earlier conclusions, Steidl displayed the kind of professional integrity that is expected within the scientific community.

Paul Steidl is to be commended for his attempt to alert the readers of the *Quarterly* to the fact that the credibility of earlier reports regarding solar contraction had been greatly diminished by further investigation. Unfortunately, his warnings went unheeded. Long after Steidl's letter appeared in the *Quarterly,* and long after the professional journals had published extensive papers discrediting the initial claim, references to the shrinking sun as a "scientific evidence" for a young earth continued to appear in the creationist literature. The *Impact* article by Akridge, in spite of its grievous shortcomings, had far more influence than Steidl's more critical appraisal.

Reflections on the Scientific-Creationist Approach

As this case study has illustrated, what began as a puzzling report within the professional scientific community was transformed by the scientific-creationist community into a "scientific evidence" purporting to substantiate their recent-creation scenario. But this transformation from scientific puzzle to recent-creation evidence carried, we believe, too high a price tag.

In order to make the shrinking sun concept function as a young-earth evidence, numerous principles of good scientific practice had to be breached: one preliminary report—a report soon discredited—had to be granted far greater weight than several substantial reports subsequently published; the principles of meaningful extrapolation had to be violated; and the relevance of several important phenomena and much readily accessible data had to be disregarded. The shrinking sun report, as it propagated through the recent-creationist literature, lost contact with the critical evaluation and continuing investigation performed with competence and integrity by the community of professional scientists. And, having lost this vital connection, the solar shrinkage report became the "legend of the shrinking sun"—the vehicle of misinformation and unwarranted conclusions.

Postscript

The substance of this chapter was published as an article in the September 1986 issue of the *Journal of the American Scientific Affiliation.*[34] In the March 1987 issue of the *Creation Research Society Quarterly,*

Thomas G. Barnes published a rebuttal to this material.[35] In the rebuttal Barnes clings to the idea of solar shrinkage for the duration of the sun's history. Our references to published criticisms of Eddy and Boornazian's 1979 report were characterized by Barnes as "nit-picking" and as providing "nothing of quantitative value." Eddy's 1984 report of the recent *increase* in solar diameter was ignored entirely. And, very interestingly, our criticism of the unrestrained (and therefore meaningless) extrapolation employed in the creation-science literature to reach a recent-creation conclusion was uncontested, in fact, not even acknowledged. Barnes's conclusion: *"The case for a shrinking sun still holds."*

FOOTPRINTS
ON THE
DUSTY MOON

4

T
HE EAGLE *HAS LANDED." IT WAS THE VOICE OF NEIL*
Armstrong, relayed by radio from his spacecraft on the
surface of the moon to the many millions of us on earth
who were excited by man's exploration of space.[1] This was
an exhilarating and historic moment—July 20, 1969—cap-
ping a tremendous effort over several years. U.S. President John F.
Kennedy had laid out the agenda eight years earlier. The United
States, he said, "should commit itself to achieving the goal, before this
decade is out, of landing a man on the moon and returning him safely
to earth."[2]

About six and a half hours after landing, Armstrong descended the
ladder of the lunar module to the moon's surface. The event was well
documented by radio and television. Again, Armstrong's words, as

reported in the December 1969 issue of *National Geographic Magazine:*

I'm at the foot of the ladder. The LM (lunar module) footpads are only depressed in the surface about one or two inches, although the surface appears to be very, very fine grained, as you get close to it. It's almost like a powder. Now and then it's very fine. I'm going to step off the LM now. That's one small step for man, one giant leap for mankind.

Moments later, while taking his first steps on the lunar surface, he noted:

The surface is fine and powdery. I can—I can pick it up loosely with my toe. It does adhere in fine layers like powdered charcoal to the sole and sides of my boots. I only go in a small fraction of an inch, maybe an eighth of an inch, but I can see the footprints of my boots and the treads in the fine sandy particles.

And a little later, while picking up samples of rocks and fine material, he said:

This is very interesting. It's a very soft surface, but here and there where I plug with the contingency sample collector, I run into a very hard surface, but it appears to be very cohesive material of the same sort. I'll try to get a rock in here. Here's a couple.

One of the photos in that *National Geographic* article shows astronaut Aldrin carrying some instruments over the surface of the moon, and the caption of the photo noted that "Aldrin makes three-to-four-inch-deep tracks as he bypasses a crater."

And so the manned exploration of the moon began. Since that initial touchdown there have been five more manned lunar landings, culminating in Apollo-17 in December 1972.

So too, apparently, began the claim that the moon must be young (not more than 10,000-15,000 years old) because, "If the moon were billions of years old, it should have accumulated extensive layers of space dust,"[3] but "the fact is that astronauts found the layer to be only about 1/8 to 3 inches in thickness. 3 inches of dust could easily have been deposited in 8,000 years."[4]

Before we can evaluate the claim that, on the basis of the thickness of its surface-dust layer, the moon must be young, we need to examine the history of the professional scientific community's investigation of lunar dust. Two questions are particularly relevant: (1) What estimates or measurements have been made to ascertain the rate at which dust accumulates on the moon? (2) What amount of dust was actually found on its surface?

The Rate of Dust Accumulation

Pulverized material on the moon's surface comes from two sources: (1) the meteoritic material which falls onto the moon's surface from space and (2) the grinding up of lunar rocks by various processes, including the fall of meteorites. These two phenomena will be discussed separately.

Several estimates of the rate at which meteorites fall to earth were published from 1930-50 based on visual observations of meteors and meteorite falls. The results, summarized in 1950 by Buddhue,[5] ranged from 26 metric tons per year to 45,000 tons per year. (One metric ton is 2200 pounds, slightly larger than one U.S. ton.) In 1956 Watson[6] included consideration of smaller particles falling to earth, with estimates based on faint telescopic meteors, radiometeors (meteors detected by radar) and on the still finer dust particles that produce the zodiacal light. Watson estimated a total accumulation rate on earth of 300,000-3,000,000 tons per year. In 1956 Opik[7] estimated 250,000 tons per year (on earth), and in 1959 Whipple[8] estimated 700,000 tons per year, both estimates including a consideration of the zodiacal light.

A considerably different technique was used by Hans Petterson[9] in 1960. Microscopic spheres of magnetic materials had been found in ocean sediments, and most investigators concluded that these were produced by meteoritic material falling onto the earth. Petterson collected dust samples from the air at the summit of Haleakala, Hawaii, in order to capture meteoritic dust with as little contamination of terrestrial material as possible. He made a further correction for contamination by terrestrial material on the basis of chemical composition. He estimated that 14 million tons of meteoritic material fall onto the earth each year.

More reliable and direct observation of micrometeors became possible with the launching of orbiting spacecraft. The earliest detectors employed microphones that used the sound of meteor impacts to determine the particle flux (number of particles per square centimeter per second) and the mass of each impacting particle. The initial results showed large variations from satellite to satellite, and sometimes from time to time for the same satellite.

Another type of detector, put into use somewhat later, detected micrometeors by their penetration through a thin metal foil or membrane. The flux of micrometeors observed by these detectors was from 10 to 100 times less than that obtained from the microphone data. The results of both types of measurement were reported at a symposium on meteor orbits and dust held August 9-13, 1965, sponsored by NASA and by the Smithsonian Institution.[10] The differences were noted, but the discrepancies were not yet explained in any of the papers presented at that meeting.

The discrepancy was resolved, however, soon after that symposium. The microphone results indicated an erroneously high flux value because the data were contaminated with sounds from mechanical movement and from thermal expansion and contraction of the spacecraft and the detectors; additional spurious counts could be attributed to solar flare and cosmic ray activity.[11]

The mechanisms producing the zodiacal light are not yet well understood, so calculations of the micrometeor flux based on the zodiacal light are considered unreliable; the results of those calculations are too dependent on which model is used for the calculations.

Additional measurements of particle flux have been based on impact pits in the windows of many spacecraft (including the Apollo vehicles) and parts of the Surveyor-3 spacecraft which were returned to earth by Apollo-12 astronauts after Surveyor-3 had been exposed to micrometeorite bombardment for 31 months on the moon. These measurements plus continuing measurements by penetration detectors and by modified microphone detectors have provided the most reliable estimates for the accumulation of meteoritic material on earth and moon. Gault (1972) reports 20,000 tons per year on earth,[12] Millman (1973) gives 10,000-20,000 tons,[13] and Hughes (1978) gives 16,000 tons.[14] Petterson's 1960 estimate based on atmospheric dust is a thousand times higher than these results; Petterson's samples were apparently contaminated with far more terrestrial dust than he had accounted for.

To compute a reasonable estimate for the accumulation of meteoritic dust on the moon we divide the earth's accumulation rate of 16,000 tons per year by 16 for the moon's smaller surface area, divide again by 2 for the moon's smaller gravitational force, yielding an accumulation rate of about 500 tons per year on the moon. *By best current estimates, then, the accumulation of meteoritic dust on the moon would contribute a layer less than one centimeter thick in four billion years.* Because the intense cratering in the lunar highlands indicates a considerably higher rate of fall for large meteorites early in the moon's history, before the formation of the lunar maria, the accumulation of meteoritic dust on the highlands would be somewhat greater.

The second source of pulverized material on the moon is the erosion of exposed lunar rocks by various processes. One of the most striking features of the moon viewed through a telescope is that much of the surface is pocked with craters, some of them very large. Initially volcanic activity was thought responsible for the craters, with meteorite impacts being suggested as an alternative mechanism. By about 1950, however, most investigators were convinced that meteorite impact was the major mechanism involved.[15] Such impacts would pulverize large amounts of rock and scatter the fragments over the moon's surface. Radar studies of the moon were consistent with the conclusion that the surface was made of fine particles. Everyone agreed that the moon's surface was probably covered with a layer of pulverized material, but there were at that time no very good ways to estimate its actual thickness.

In 1956 R. A. Lyttleton suggested that ultraviolet light and x-rays from the sun could slowly erode the surface of exposed rocks on the moon.[16] He suggested further that the dust particles produced by that erosion might be kept in agitated motion by heat energy and by cosmic ray particles so that there would be a slow "flow" of fluffy dust to lower elevations on the moon. This flow of dust would keep the rocks exposed to continuing erosion, providing a layer of dust which might be "several miles deep."[17]

Lyttleton noted that the lunar maria and the floors of large craters appear to be quite smooth and that the rims of many craters appear rounded and smoothed out rather than sharp. He suggested that the flow of a thick, fluffy dust layer would explain those smooth surface features. Thomas Gold also suggested (1955) that the moon is probably covered with loose dust which could present a serious hazard to any spacecraft landing on the moon.[18]

Fred L. Whipple, on the other hand, argued in 1959 that the dust layer would be firm and compact.[19] He noted that particles in vacuum tend to adhere to each other. He also suggested that bombardment by electrically charged particles from the sun (the solar wind) would produce "sputtering" and chemical changes, which would tend to cement the particles together. He predicted that humans and vehicles would have no trouble landing on and moving across the moon's surface. By 1964 Salisbury and Smalley wrote:

> It is concluded that the lunar surface is covered with a layer of rubble of highly variable thickness and block size. The rubble in turn is mantled with a layer of highly porous dust which is thin over topographic highs, but thick in depressions. The dust has a complex surface and a significant, but not strong, coherence.[20]

When NASA engineers were designing spacecraft for landing on the moon, they considered some possible designs for landing on a thick layer of fluffy dust. By the time the designs were completed, however, they were convinced that the surface would be firm. The foot pads for Surveyor and for Apollo were designed for landing on a relatively firm surface.

The Thickness of the Lunar Regolith

Well, so much for the predictions. What did we find when we got there? The soft landings of Luna IX and Surveyor I (1966) confirmed that the surface is firm and compacted. The Surveyor sample scoop was able to dig a trench a few inches deep. As Neil Armstrong (Apollo-11) observed, the upper part is quite soft, but it is very firm just below the surface. Apollo-11 astronauts, using a hand-operated corer, were able to get a core sample only about 5 inches deep. On later landings electric coring drills were used to obtain cores: Apollo-15 yielded 270 cm. (approximately 8 ft. 10 in.) deep and Apollo-17 yielded 294 cm. (approximately 9 ft. 8 in.) deep.

The layer of pulverized material on the moon isn't usually called moon dust; it is called lunar regolith, and the fine materials in it are sometimes referred to as lunar soil. The fine material is quite uniform throughout the depths sampled, although some layering was observed in Apollo-15 and -17 cores, probably produced by deposits from different cratering events. There are rocks of various sizes found throughout the regolith. On the basis of chemical analysis of core samples, we know that the meteoritic component is mixed uniformly throughout the depth sampled. The meteoritic component makes up about 1.5% of the regolith on the lunar maria, and perhaps up to 10% on the lunar highlands.[21]

The astronauts on Apollo-17 conducted seismic tests near their landing site to measure the thickness of the regolith. The thickness in that region was found to range from 6.2 meters (20 ft.) to 39.6 meters (120 ft.).[22] Estimates of the thickness elsewhere are based on photographs taken by astronauts of the walls of craters and rills, and on the depths of some of the craters which have penetrated to bedrock. Estimates are that the regolith averages four or five meters thick

on the lunar maria, and about twice that thick on the lunar highlands.[23]

Evaluating the Young-Moon Claim

We now resume our evaluation of the young-moon claim by taking
a careful look at the way in which the data and argumentation are
presented in several representative publications.

The handbook which accompanies the *ORIGINS* film series (1983)
states the claim in these words:

> Interplanetary dust, meteors and meteorites are the source of a
> great deal of dust which regularly falls on both the moon and
> Earth. Dr. Slusher points out that this dust is being deposited on
> the moon at a rate of at least 14,300,000 tons per year (and perhaps
> at a rate 10 times that amount). After 4.5 to 5 billion years there
> should be a 440 to 990 foot thick layer of dust on the moon. Before
> the first moon landings, evolutionary scientists were concerned
> that landing astronauts might sink out of sight in all that lunar dust!
> The fact is that astronauts found the layer to be only about 1/8 to
> 3 inches in thickness. 3 inches of dust could easily have been
> deposited in 8,000 years.

No references are provided for the accumulation rate given nor for
the reported amount of dust found. The accumulation rate given for
the moon is nearly equal to Petterson's 1960 estimate for the earth.
Though this handbook was published in 1983, the authors of the
claim apparently had not given any consideration to other estimates
contemporary with Petterson's nor to the much lower estimates published since 1972 and supported by much better evidence. The "1/8
to 3 inches" of dust reported here appears to be based on conversations of Apollo-11 astronauts with NASA Houston Control, and no
consideration was given to the numerous additional measurements
and observations which confirm the presence of a considerably
thicker layer.

The earliest publication we have located which claims that the moon must be young because only a little dust was found on its surface is an article, "Some Astronomical Evidences for a Youthful Solar System," by Harold S. Slusher in the *Creation Research Society Quarterly*, June 1971. Slusher presents the claim in these words:

Estimates of the influx range considerably with different investigators. The Swedish geophysicist, Petterson, estimates 14,300,000 tons of meteoric dust come onto the surface of the earth per year. In five billion years there should be a layer of dust 54 feet in thickness on the earth if it were to lie undisturbed.

From the reports of the lunar landings the accumulation of dust on the surface of the moon is very small (not much more than 1/8 inch).[3] The moon moves through the same region of space that the earth does and consequently should have about the same influx of meteoric dust as the earth. N.A.S.A. scientists were worried that a lunar ship would sink down into the postulated huge amount of dust that should have accumulated on the surface in about 4.5 billion years of assumed time.

Also, in the "sea" areas, where the lunar ships landed, there should have accumulated more dust than elsewhere on the moon. Yet the amount of dust is amazingly small. What could have happened to all the dust?

Although more data and calculations are needed to substantiate this conclusion, from the absence of dust, we may deduce a short period of time for accumulation, and thus a young age for the moon. If the earth is about the same age as the moon (as the Scriptures assert and as some astronomers suggest), then the earth is also young.[24]

The reference [3] given in that article for the reported 1/8 inch of dust is the El Paso [Texas] *Herald-Post*, July 21, 1969. This claim, which apparently began on the basis of a daily newspaper report, has continued to be published by young-earth advocates until the present time.

The list of evidences compiled by Walter T. Brown, Jr., includes the following argument:

> If the moon were billions of years old, it should have accumulated extensive layers of space dust—possibly a mile in thickness. Before instruments were placed on the moon, NASA was very concerned that our astronauts would sink into a sea of dust. This did not happen; there is very little space dust on the moon. Conclusion: the moon is young.[25]

The reference given is to Petterson, but the language "possibly a mile in thickness" is more likely from Lyttleton's 1956 estimate. The claim gives no consideration to the large amount of data that had been published by 1981.

The January 1982 issue of *Bible-Science Newsletter* presents the young-moon claim in the form of a ("scientific") creationist prediction that was confirmed by observation:

> Evolutionists complain that creationism is not real science because it cannot make scientific predictions. Making such predictions is important for science as it attempts to put together an accurate world-view, in order to provide benefit to man. The truth is, of course, that creationist science does make predictions. Some of the predictions are so startling to evolutionists that they immediately discount them as predictions until they come true!
>
> One such case in point is the often repeated story about the depth of the moon dust. When William Overn, now serving as Co-Director of the Bible-Science Association, was working for the Univac Division of Sperry Rand on the television sub-system for Mariner IV, he had opportunity for exchanges with the men at the Jet Propulsion Laboratory who were working on the Apollo Moon program. In 1962 the amount of dust in space had been accurately measured. Assuming that the moon was 4.5 billion years old, Apollo scientists were concerned that there would be a dangerously deep layer of dust on the moon. It was even feared that a lander might disappear below the soft accumulation, even with the wide feet which were designed for it.

Since Mr. Overn knew, as a creationist, that the moon could not be over ten-thousand years old, he also knew that the dust encountered there could only represent a ten-thousand year, or less, accumulation. He told the Apollo scientists at the Jet Propulsion Laboratory that they should not worry about finding more than ten-thousand years worth of dust. They were so sure that this creationist prediction was wrong that a bet was established. Of course we all know, now, that the astronauts found less than a quarter of an inch of dust, just as predicted!

Evolutionist-believing scientists spent some time searching for their missing dust, but never had any success in finding it. They have never been able to explain the lack of dust and have finally given up trying. In one recent debate, the evolutionist suggested that the original space dust measurements, taken in 1962, were inaccurate. But he had no explanation as to why these readings might be considered to be inaccurate.

Here we have one of many excellent examples of the creationist approach which has led to a scientific prediction which proved accurate. Even more important is that the outcome of the prediction remains a total enigma to those holding the evolutionistic world-view.

One hardly knows where to begin in evaluating such a report. The statements about the amount of dust predicted and the amount found reflect both gross misinformation and ignorance of research results published before 1982. The conclusions presented in this account appear to be based on hearsay, or on secondary and tertiary sources. No references are provided, and there is no evidence that any of the primary technical literature on the subject was consulted. Nor is there any indication that the author consulted even the popular accounts of the Apollo program, such as those found in publications like *National Geographic Magazine*.

The comments about scientists "searching for their missing dust" are pure fancy; they found plenty of "dust," in good agreement with what might reasonably have been expected. (This is not to deny that some individual scientists had predicted more than was found, but by 1969-72 those high estimates were no longer considered reasonable.) The anecdote about William Overn may well be true, although it is likely that NASA engineers were influenced far more by Fred L. Whipple's arguments in 1959 than they were by William Overn's reassurances in 1962.

The sixth-grade science textbook *Observing God's World,* published by A Beka Book Publications in 1978, also makes the claim that the moon must be young:

> Space explorers have discovered that a thin layer of meteoritic dust covers the hard crust of lunar soil. This discovery came as a surprise to many scientists who expected a very deep dust layer. Evolutionists predicted a thick layer of dust because they believed it would have accumulated over billions of years. The very thin layer of dust indicates that the moon is just several thousand years old, which supports the creationist theory that the universe is very young.[26]

The misinformation about the amount of dust expected and the amount found that was noted above in other publications is here being passed along to schoolchildren. The confusion between meteoritic dust and lunar soil may have come from a misinterpretation of the conversations of the Apollo-11 astronauts. The looser layer on top and the firmer material below are actually the same type of material, that is, pulverized lunar rock with a little meteoritic material mixed throughout. The list of consultants for the A Beka Book science textbooks includes two engineers and a chemist as well as a physician and a pharmacist. It is apparent, however, that they did not do their "homework" in evaluating the scientific accuracy of the moon-dust claim printed in this sixth-grade text.

The widely distributed book *Scientific Creationism* presents the thinly dusted young moon picture in its 1974 edition as follows:

> It is known that there is essentially a constant rate of cosmic dust

particles entering the earth's atmosphere from space and then gradually settling to the earth's surface. The best measurements of this influx have been made by Hans Petterson, who obtained the figure of 14 million tons per year. This amounts to 14×10^{19} pounds in 5 billion years. If we assume the density of compacted dust is, say, 140 pounds per cubic foot, this corresponds to a volume of 10^{18} cubic feet. Since the earth has a surface area of approximately 5.5×10^{15} square feet, this seems to mean that there should have accumulated during the 5-billion-year age of the earth, a layer of meteoritic dust approximately 182 feet thick all over the world!

There is not the slightest sign of such a dust layer anywhere of course. On the moon's surface it should be at least as thick, but the astronauts found no sign of it (before the moon landings, there was considerable fear that the men would sink into the dust when they arrived on the moon, but no comment has apparently ever been made by the authorities as to why it wasn't there as anticipated).[27]

The foreword and the back-cover description of our copy of *Scientific Creationism,* 1975 printing, characterize the book as having been "prepared by an outstanding team of creationist scientists" and as being "thoroughly documented and authoritative." The book has been widely used and quoted as an authoritative source of information for readers who have had little or no scientific training. Yet, quoting the dust accumulation rate by Petterson as a product of "the best measurements of this influx" fails to take into account the many other measurements that have been made, especially by satellite penetration sensors, which are considered to be the most reliable by workers in the field and which were available well before *Scientific Creationism* was first published.

The statement that "the astronauts found no sign" of a dust layer on the moon fails to take into account those many results of the Apollo program which had reported the thickness and the character of that layer. *Scientific Creationism* has gone through twelve printings, the most recent one being a 1985 updated and expanded version, but *no change* has been made in the claims related to moon dust. Apparently no consideration is being given to modifying or relinquishing that claim in spite of the many evidences that the claim is founded on erroneous information.

There are some patterns in the claims that the moon must be young which should be noted. For this claim to be credible, there must be *much* less dust found on the moon than would be consistent with known rates of dust accumulation over 4.5 billion years. All the claims of young-moon advocates assert that very little or no dust was found on the moon by Apollo explorations. This assertion is plainly shown to be false by many reports of the results of the Apollo program which have been published in the technical literature, as well as in accounts found in popular publications such as *National Geographic.*

Anyone who seriously tries to find out how much pulverized material was found on the moon by the Apollo investigations can easily confirm that a thick layer was found. In spite of this, however, the assertion that little or none was found has persisted for a dozen or more years after the Apollo flights. The failure to take into account the published data pertinent to the topic being discussed is a clear failure to live up to the codes of thoroughness and integrity that ought to characterize professional science.

Young-moon claims would also be supported if the rates of meteoritic dust accumulation and the rates of lunar rock erosion were found to be very high, so that the accumulation expected over 4.5 billion years would greatly exceed what was found. The reference for meteoritic dust accumulation most commonly quoted by young-moon advocates is Petterson's 1960 value. Apparently no consideration is given to the more recent direct measurements by satellite-borne instruments, which are considered by knowledgeable researchers in the field to be the most reliable means of data collection currently available. Petterson's estimate is about 1000 times higher than the best recent estimate given by Hughes in 1978 (see ref. 14).

Young-moon advocates most commonly quote Lyttleton's 1956

book for a pre-Apollo estimate of lunar rock erosion and accumulation of erosional dust. Lyttleton's estimate is the highest that we are aware of in the professional scientific literature. More recent laboratory studies and results of the Apollo program show that estimate to be much too high. The agents of erosion which Lyttleton suggested, x-rays and ultraviolet rays, are not effective in rock erosion on the moon. The most effective agent of erosion on the moon is the fall of micrometeors, and the rate of erosion on exposed rock surfaces is only about 0.3 millimeters per million years[28]—much less than Lyttleton's estimate of a few hundred inches per million years.

Furthermore, after a thin layer of erosional fragments has covered the surface, the micrometeors no longer produce any additional erosion. Only the larger impacts will produce cratering and bring more rocks to the surface, where they will be subject to further erosion. Although very precise rates of cratering and erosion are still not available, the thickness of the regolith is close to what would be expected if the moon is about 4.5 billion years old.[29] Again, the failure of young-moon advocates to consider pertinent data that have been published indicates a failure to follow expected procedure for professional science.

It is easy to understand that sixth-grade teachers would not be in touch with the current professional scientific literature, although they certainly have access to popular publications such as *National Geographic Magazine* and *Scientific American*. In contrast, there is little excuse for writers with advanced degrees in scientific fields who do not keep themselves informed of technical publications on topics about which they choose to write.

The persistence of young-moon advocates in quoting accumulation rates from Petterson and Lyttleton, even though those estimates have been conclusively discredited as being vastly too high, demonstrates a failure to employ the best-published data on that topic. The persistence in asserting that little or no dust was found on the moon, even though core samples, seismic tests and photographic evidence conclusively demonstrated the presence of a thick regolith, constitutes a serious failure to consider either the technical literature or the popular accounts of the Apollo program.

The claim that a thick layer of dust should be expected on the surface of the moon, and the claim that not more than a few inches of dust were found on the surface of the moon, are contradicted by an abundance of published evidence. The continuing publication of those claims by young-earth advocates constitutes an intolerable violation of the standards of professional integrity that should characterize the work of natural scientists.

TIMELESS TALES FROM THE SALTY SEA

5

"**A**LL STREAMS FLOW INTO THE SEA, YET THE SEA IS never full. To the place the streams come from, there they return again."

So says the Preacher in Ecclesiastes 1:7. But, to add a technical note to the Preacher's observation, the streams leave most of their salts in the sea each time they repeat this cycle. As water flows over or through the rocks and the soil to get to the streams, it dissolves numerous minerals and carries them down to the sea. Calcium, iron, sodium, chlorides, sulfates, carbonates and a host of other materials are carried into the oceans by earth's streams, and most of those "salts" are left in the oceans when the water evaporates and returns to the land as rain or snow, ready to repeat the salt transportation cycle.

Late last century John Joly thought that he could determine the age of the oceans by comparing the rate at which sodium is carried into the ocean with the amount of sodium salt which had already accumulated there. Using data collected by others as well as by himself, he obtained information on the amount of water that each of the earth's major rivers annually delivered to the ocean and on the average concentration of salt in those rivers. He also used estimates of the total volume of water in the oceans, and measurements of the concentration of sodium in ocean water. In 1899 he published his conclusion that the age of the earth's oceans is between 80 and 90 million years.[1] Notice that this is an estimate of the age of the oceans and not of the earth itself, though Joly thought the age of the earth was close to the age of its oceans.

The Determination of Residence Times

Since 1899 a great deal of work has been done in measuring the concentration of many materials in ocean water and in the streams that flow into the ocean. Furthermore, much progress has been made in trying to understand the several processes that go on within the oceans and at the oceans' boundaries (floor, shore and surface) which *remove* those materials from the ocean water.

For example, coral reefs are constructed primarily of calcium carbonate which has been extracted from ocean water by coral animals, thereby removing calcium and carbon from ocean water; deep ocean sediments contain large quantities of skeletal remains of microscopic organisms (plankton, radiolarians, etc.) which have extracted calcium carbonate or silicon dioxide from ocean water to make those skeletons, thereby removing calcium, carbon and silicon from ocean water; some elements adhere to the surfaces of clay particles which settle to the ocean floor, thus effectively removing those elements from solution in the ocean water. The global ocean is a highly complex system, and while much progress has been made in our endeavor to understand it, still many questions remain for which our tentative answers are neither very precise nor very certain. The study of all these processes continues.

Some of the processes that remove certain materials from the ocean water occur continuously, such as the settling of clay particles to the ocean floor, carrying with them those materials that adhere to the surfaces of such small particles. Some salt-removing processes must have occurred only episodically, such as the evaporation which deposited the thick layers of rock salt in Michigan, New York, Kansas and many other parts of the world. Many of these phenomena are interrelated, so that a change in one of them will affect the entire complex network. And many of these processes are also affected by changes in ocean conditions such as temperature and acidity.

Some dissolved salts stay in the ocean water a long time before being removed. Some are removed quickly by reactions which incorporate them into the solid particles that form the ocean floor sediment. The average amount of time that an atom of an element remains dissolved or suspended in ocean water is called the *residence time* of that element in ocean water. Several measurements have been made to determine the residence times of as many elements as possible. An extensive table of those data was published in the two-volume work *Chemical Oceanography* in 1965.[2]

The residence time for an element depends on how soluble the various chemical forms of that element are, on how reactive the element is in the ocean environment and on several other factors. The residence times range from 100 years for aluminum to 260 million years for sodium. Interesting enough, a few elements, such as boron and bromine, exhibit concentrations in ocean water that are even higher than would have accumulated there at present-day rates in 4.5 billion years; residence times for those elements are not included in *Chemical Oceanography*. In the context of all of these considerations, it should be evident that Joly's calculations did not provide a measure of the *age* of the ocean; they merely yielded the residence time for sodium (with a result somewhat too low).

Confusing Residence Time for Age

The residence times listed in *Chemical Oceanography* are considerably less than the age of the earth as determined by methods based on radioactivity. That information has been used by some young-earth advocates as the basis of their claim that the earth cannot be as old as the results of radioactive dating indicate. In *Scientific Creationism*, for example, the residence times of several elements are listed,[3] the values being quoted from *Chemical Oceanography*.

The column of time values given in *Scientific Creationism*, however, has the heading "Years to Accumulate in Ocean from River Inflow" instead of the more appropriate one, "Residence Times." Accompanying comments about those times refer to them *as if* they were calculations of the *age* of the oceans, which they are not. We read, for example:

> The significant thing to note, however, is that in every case the calculated apparent age is vastly less than the supposed 5 billion year age of the earth.[4]

And, after noting the wide range of "apparent ages,"

> This situation is difficult to understand if the earth's lithosphere and hydrosphere are indeed billions of years old, and if uniformitarianism is a valid assumption in geochronology.[5]

These comments in *Scientific Creationism* and similar comments in other literature that advocates the young-earth hypothesis[6] are apparently based on a substantial misunderstanding. Residence times are *not* useful for measuring the age of the oceans nor of the earth. That they cannot be used for measuring age is already evident from the fact that residence times of several elements are less than a thousand years, and we all know that the oceans are older than that. If residence times were ages, those that are less than 6000 years would present as urgent a problem to young-earth advocates as they would to old-earth advocates, and those that are higher than about 15,000 years should present an even greater problem to young-earth advocates. But residence times of elements in the ocean are not ages.

One young-earth advocate, Melvin A. Cook, recognizes that ocean salts do not provide a way of measuring ages:

> The validity of the application of total salt in the ocean in the determination of age turned out to have a very simple answer in the fact shown by Goldschmidt [1954] that it is in steady state and therefore useless as a means of determining the age of the oceans.[7]

The closest that residence times come to indicating the age of anything is the reasonable conclusion that the *highest* residence time for any element (260 million years for sodium) would be a *minimum* age for the ocean. Even Joly took note in 1899 that elements with residence times less than that of sodium are removed from ocean water by various processes, and therefore could not be used to measure the age of the oceans.

Ignoring Salt-Removal Phenomena

Under certain conditions the salts dissolved in ocean water may be removed by evaporation of the water. The writers of *Scientific Creationism* claim that this does not happen.

> The attempt to explain the small amounts of these elements in terms of precipitation on the ocean bottom will not work. One of the world's leading oceanographers, P. H. Kuenen, said:
>
>> Under normal conditions, sea water is not supersaturated with any product, and circulation is automatically set up in areas of excessive concentrations.
>>
>> Chemicals normally do not precipitate out of solution until the water is first supersaturated with them.[8]

Looking at the context of Kuenen's remarks is very instructive for us. Immediately following the sentence quoted above, he wrote:

> However, if circulation is restricted, e.g. in shallow water or inland seas and gulfs with constricted entrances, evaporation in a dry climate will lead to abnormal concentrations. These may either cause purely inorganic precipitation or may combine with bacterial action to bring about precipitation. Calcium carbonate, gypsum or

anhydrite are then deposited, and if the process continues, various other salts may be formed (see Chapters 16 and 19).[9]

An example of evaporite formation from relatively recent times is described in the article "When the Mediterranean Dried Up" published in *Scientific American* in December 1972.[10]

Because of evaporite formation and other removal processes, the rates of influx of various elements into the earth's oceans clearly do not measure the *age* of anything. Defenders of the young-earth hypothesis, however, continue to speak as if influx rates could be employed in that way. A flyer published in 1981 by ICR Midwest, entitled "Evidence that Implies a Young Earth and Solar System," lists fourteen evidences compiled by Walter T. Brown. One of those entries states:

> The rate at which elements such as copper, gold, tin, lead, silicon, mercury, uranium, and nickel are entering the oceans is very rapid when compared with the small quantities of these elements already in the oceans. Therefore, the oceans must be very much younger than a million years.

Brown gives no consideration to the processes which are removing these elements from ocean water, in spite of the fact that much literature has been published on the subject. In *The Biblical Basis for Modern Science*, Henry Morris lists 68 "Uniformitarian Estimates" for the age of the earth.[11] Of the 68 entries in that list, 32 are based on rates of influx of various elements into the oceans. Residence times are erroneously labeled "age."

When Relevant Information Is Disregarded

Now let's try to step back from the details a couple of paces and reflect on what has been happening in ocean science and in the young-earth claim that we have been discussing.

The organized, scientific study of ocean water and of the ocean environment has been going on for more than a century. In the 1840s and 1850s, Matthew F. Maury undertook and directed studies of ocean currents, water temperatures and weather on the oceans in preparing comprehensive navigation charts.[12] He supervised measurements of ocean depths and collected samples of ocean-floor sediments in the course of preparing plans for laying a trans-Atlantic telegraph cable. The chemistry of ocean water and the chemical behavior of the salts in ocean water have also been the subject of study for a long time. An early summary of the average composition of the salts dissolved in ocean water from several different locations was provided by Dittmar in 1884.[13]

By 1942 Sverdrup and his colleagues published the results of a comprehensive study of the ocean and its processes, giving a thorough account of the behavior of elements being added to and being removed from ocean water.[14] In 1954 Goldschmidt provided data and discussion supporting the conclusion that the dissolved material in ocean water is in an equilibrium state, being added and removed at equal rates.[15] *Chemical Oceanography,* published in 1965 and revised in 1975, includes extensive discussions of the processes by which elements are removed from ocean water, although those parts of the work appear to have been disregarded by the young-earth advocates who quote from this book in *Scientific Creationism* and elsewhere.

Immense amounts of additional measurements and new information have been obtained through the studies of the International Geophysical Year (July 1957 to December 1958) and through the Deep Sea Drilling Project (begun in 1968). The ocean floors have been mapped. We have obtained many drill-core samples of deep ocean sediments. And the processes of ocean-floor spreading and plate tectonics have come to be understood and described in considerable detail.[16] The chemical behavior of ocean water and the processes of sedimentation are much better characterized than they were twenty years ago.

The 1975 revision of *Chemical Oceanography* includes two chapters with extensive discussion of sedimentation in the ocean.[17] Recent textbooks in water chemistry[18] and in ocean science[19] include discussions of sedimentation processes in the ocean. An article has appeared in *Scientific American* on the subject.[20] All of this recent study supports the conclusion that the oceans constitute an equilibrium system, with materials being removed at the same rate as they are being added. In no way can the rates of influx of various elements into the ocean be used for any sort of age measurement.

Joly thought that he was computing the age of the oceans from his data in 1899, but not long after his work the first measurements of ages of rocks by radioactivity were published (1905-11).[21] Since that time radioactivity has become accepted by the professional scientific community as the basis for measuring ages of rocks and of the earth. Furthermore, we have accumulated additional data and have gained a better understanding of chemical processes in the oceans which confirm that Joly's method does *not* provide an age measurement.

Meanwhile, many young-earth advocates have continued to refer to the rate of influx of elements into the oceans *as if* they could be used as a basis for age measurement. The earliest publication which we have found which uses those influx rates to argue that the earth cannot be as old as 4.5 billion years (the age provided by radiometric methods) is *The Genesis Flood,* published in 1962. In *The Genesis Flood,* the claim is made that it is important to note that all the influx rates give an accumulation time "vastly less than 5 billion years." Nearly the same words are used in *Scientific Creationism,* published in 1974. The 1985 "Updated and Enlarged" edition of *Scientific Creationism* continues to publish those same claims. The authors of *Scientific Creationism* refer to the 1965 edition of *Chemical Oceanography* as their source of "Years to Accumulate" (actually, residence times), but they do not consider or acknowledge discussions of processes removing those elements from ocean water which are found in the same chapter as the residence times, as well as elsewhere in that work.

The writings of these young-earth advocates show no evidence of their having considered the large amount of published data supporting the conclusion that elements are continuously being removed from ocean water by various processes. There is no evidence in their writings that they are even aware of the many publications which report and discuss those removal processes, although those discussions were included in comprehensive books published before those young-earth claims were published. The authors of *Scientific Creationism* even deny that such processes can be operating, although the very publications they consulted to obtain residence times also contain extensive discussions of those processes, with references to the primary scientific papers which reported the data supporting the conclusions that those processes do operate in the ocean system. Even in 1985 the arguments presented by young-earth advocates continue to use influx rates of elements into the oceans to support their view, and those arguments have remained unchanged in spite of the accumulation of scientific data which support the conclusion that influx rates cannot be meaningfully used in that way.

As we discussed in chapter two, it is a requirement of professional integrity that a scientist give due recognition to all relevant information. Failure to do so may be sufficient warrant to discredit one's conclusions. In the specific case that we have been reviewing, the failure to distinguish between the remarkably different concepts of *residence time* and *age*, coupled with the failure to incorporate a vast amount of published information concerning processes by which sea salts are either continuously or episodically removed from ocean water, does indeed thoroughly discredit the conclusion that oceanic salt content supports the young-earth hypothesis. The 4.5 billion year chronology of earth history is in no way weakened or disqualified by an appeal to the salt content of terrestrial oceans.

MAKING MYSTERIES OUT OF MISSING ROCK

6

SCIENTIFIC CREATIONISTS HAVE REPEATEDLY claimed that geological field evidence can best be explained in terms of a recent creation and a catastrophic global deluge. That claim has been made specifically for the Grand Canyon of northern Arizona. At least three similar "flood geology" models have been proposed for the Grand Canyon, and, according to Walter Lang, "All three, or combinations thereof, are permissible on the basis of Scripture. . . . Any of these models provides explanations which are superior to the uniformitarian model which claims that the bottom rocks are two billion years old and that the Colorado River, eroding at its present rate, carved the canyon over a period of from seven million to 36 million years."[1]

To test flood geology's claim to superiority, we examine some illustrative aspects of the geology of the Grand Canyon. For several reasons, the Grand Canyon provides an ideal test case of the merits of the geological theories of scientific creationism: (1) many geological claims have been made about this area by scientific creationists; (2) the region is familiar to many laypersons; (3) the rocks are very well exposed; and (4) the geology is relatively simple and has been very thoroughly documented.[2]

The Grand Canyon region is part of the Colorado Plateau, a major geological province that occupies large portions of Utah, Colorado, New Mexico and Arizona. The plateau consists largely of nearly horizontal layers of a variety of sedimentary rocks that are stacked on top of one another. Due to extensive erosion, the layers are now well exposed in the spectacular cliffs, mesas, buttes, spires and canyons that abound throughout the plateau. Locally the layers of the plateau have been warped into broad dome-shaped uplifts or depressed into broad basins. Where the Colorado River has eroded through the uplifts, as in Canyonlands National Park in Utah, deep canyons have formed. In northern Arizona, the river has chiseled its way down through the Kaibab-Coconino uplift to form the Grand Canyon.

In the walls of the Grand Canyon, approximately 4000 feet of superimposed horizontal strata are well exposed. Figure 3 summarizes the names of the formations that are exposed in the walls of this magnificent canyon. Also included are the approximate thicknesses of the formations, the standard geological periods assigned to these formations, and their approximate age in years as accepted by the professional geological community.[3] The horizontal strata toward the bottom of the canyon rest on top of tilted rocks designated as the Unkar and Chuar Groups.[4]

These rocks in turn rest on highly deformed igneous and metamorphic rocks[5]—known as the Vishnu Schist and Zoroaster Granite. The spatial relationships among the Tapeats Sandstone, lowermost of the horizontal layers, the Unkar Group, and the Vishnu Schist and Zoroaster Granite are shown schematically in figure 3. As indicated by

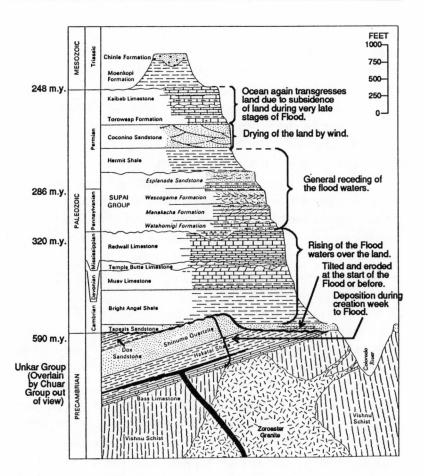

Figure 3. Schematic diagram of the stratigraphy of the Grand Canyon modified from McKee (1982). The ages in years of selected boundaries are those of Harland et al. (1982). Included for comparison is an interpretation of the geology in terms of a flood model.

the diagram, some of the geologic systems, for example, the Ordovician and Silurian,[6] are absent from the Grand Canyon. Figure 3 also presents (in the notation to the right) the elements of a deluge model as suggested by scientific creationists.[7]

Scientific creationists have expended considerable effort in studying the Grand Canyon. Recently they established a Grand Canyon research center near Flagstaff, Arizona. For several years both the Bible-Science Association and the Institute for Creation Research have conducted seminars and field trips at the Grand Canyon. Articles about the Grand Canyon have been featured frequently on the pages of the *Bible-Science Newsletter*. Creationists Walter Lang and Clifford Burdick have each published booklets about the geology of the Grand Canyon.[8]

Among the specific claims about the Grand Canyon region that creationists have made are these:

1. Most of the horizontal layers exposed in the walls of the Canyon were deposited during Noah's flood.[9] The uppermost layers, like the Coconino Sandstone, may have been deposited during the waning stages of the flood.

2. All "kinds"[10] of life forms were created by God a few thousand years ago. The fossils in the Grand Canyon strata were formed as the flood destroyed and buried successive habitats containing the animals and plants originally created by God a few centuries earlier.

3. The Canyon itself was formed when huge cracks split apart the upward bulging Kaibab and Coconino Plateaus at the conclusion of the flood epoch. An enormous lake in the Colorado-Wyoming region, representing remnants of the great flood, drained catastrophically as a huge wall of water through the cracks, modifying and widening them as the draining waters eroded away the still soft, layered flood sediments now exposed in the walls of the Canyon.[11] Some creationists have postulated that the catastrophic faulting of the Kaibab uplift may have occurred about 100 years after the flood and that the layered sediments within the Canyon had already solidified.

4. The theory of evolution finds no support from the Grand Canyon because of the discovery of abundant conifer spores in several of the strata.[12] Evolutionary theory claims that conifers did not evolve until after the uppermost strata had already been deposited.

5. The usual uniformitarian explanations of the geology of the Grand Canyon are inadequate because several of the geological systems are missing from the Canyon.[13] There is no physical evidence to indicate erosion of any missing systems. The physical evidence indicates that the layers were deposited continuously.

The list above represents only a small sample of the numerous claims made in scientific-creationist literature about the Grand Canyon. Space forbids considering all of them in detail, but each is severely lacking in scientific merit. In this case study, attention is focused on the "missing rock" claim (number 5 on the list) in order to demonstrate its utter inadequacy as a criticism of the results of professional geological investigation. This claim betrays a glaring lack of familiarity with the professional literature on Grand Canyon geology. Furthermore, the flood geology approach in which this claim is employed fails to display either internal coherence or consistency with other relevant bodies of knowledge, and it lacks the predictive accuracy expected of meaningful scientific theories.

Missing Strata
Creationists apparently think that the usual explanation of the stratigraphy of the Grand Canyon given by professional geologists is incorrect because geologists claim that there are "missing strata." They repeatedly assert that geologists (whom they persist in calling "evolutionists") have a severe problem with the Grand Canyon because only "five of twelve of the geological systems" are present.

For example, one article reviewing a creationist film about the Grand Canyon points out that the film stresses the problem of "missing rocks—the Grand Canyon is regarded as a prime example of the geologic column for in the canyon more strata of the column are found than anywhere else in the world—yet more than one-half the strata are missing in the canyon. According to evolutionists, these missing rocks add up to a total of about one billion years."[14] These missing systems are thought by creationists to be devastating to the theory of evolution. The creationists claim that there are no missing strata. The Canyon walls are said to record evidence of essentially continuous sedimentation during the great flood and possibly just after it.

One representative treatment of the problem of missing strata has been provided by Gary Parker of the Institute for Creation Research. Parker says:

> Again, evolutionists have coined a term to deal with the problem: *paraconformity.* A contact line between two rock strata is called a "conformity" if the physical evidence indicates smooth continuous deposition with no time break. "Disconformity" is used where the physical evidence indicates erosion has removed part of the rock sequence. Disconformities are often represented by wavy lines in geologic diagrams, and they often appear in the field as *real* "wavy lines" in which erosion channels and stream beds can be seen cutting into the eroded rock layer. But in the case of paraconformity, there is no evidence of erosion nor any other physical evidence of a break in time. The name even means that it looks like a conformity. In fact, the only way to recognize a paraconformity is by prior commitment to evolutionary theory. There is no physical evidence. But if you believe in evolution, then you must believe there was some gap in the sequence, or else the evolutionary chain would be broken.
>
> Creationists don't need the term *paraconformity.* Creationists can simply accept the physical evidence as it's found: smooth, continuous deposition with no time break. . . . In parts of Grand Canyon, for instance, Mississippian rock rests paraconformably on Cambrian rock—a gap of 125 million years of hypothetical evolutionary time with no evidence of a time break at all. (At some

points, however, there is a disconformity between Devonian rock and Cambrian.)[15]

The same kinds of claims are found repeatedly in articles published in the *Bible-Science Newsletter*. For example, "The formation below the Mississippian, on both sides of the canyon, is the Muav. This poses a big problem for the evolutionist geologist. Here there are three layers missing: the Ordovician, the Silurian and most of the Devonian."[16]

Such a claim calls for a careful scrutiny of both the data and their interpretation. Is there physical evidence, for example, to suggest that there are "missing rocks"? Specifically, is there physical evidence for the Cambrian-Mississippian paraconformity? Or have geologists simply invented the concept of "missing layers" in order to explain away a serious difficulty for the evolutionary theory to which they have a prior commitment?

In fact there is an abundance of physical evidence to indicate that layers of rock have been eroded away and are therefore now missing. This is so even in the specific case of the Mississippian-Cambrian paraconformity that Parker cites. Furthermore, the physical evidence exists independent of any paleontological evidence that might be adduced in support of biological evolution. *Regardless of whether or not the concept of biological evolution has any validity, the geological data clearly point to the former presence of "missing rock."*

The Precambrian-Tapeats Unconformity

We consider first the buried erosional surface—known as an *unconformity*—between the Cambrian Tapeats Sandstone and the underlying Precambrian rocks. Concerning this erosional boundary, scientific creationists have claimed

> the line which divides the lower rock from the first sedimentary rock, in this case the Cambrian, is very distinct. Creationists call this "The Great Unconformity" because, as signs along the path point out, 500 million years of the geological record is missing at this

point. If you examine the border between these two layers very carefully, you will see that, according to evolutionary time scales, the Cambrian rock was laid down directly upon the lower rock, for they fit together in a perfect fit. This would lead us to believe that if the evolutionary time scale for these rocks is correct, there was absolutely no erosion on the lower rock for 500 million years! Evolutionists do say there was erosion taking place here, but that all evidences of half billion years of weathering were swept completely away![17]

Elsewhere it is said,

Then there are the Precambrian formations—Shinumo quartzite, Hakatai shale, and Bass limestone. These are dated from 500 million years to one billion years old according to the evolutionist geological column. One problem is that these formations are totally missing in certain areas of the canyon. As you hike up the Bright Angel trail, when you get within eight-tenths of a mile of Indian Gardens, you see the Tapeats immediately on top of the Vishnu schist which is Proterozoic and dated one billion years or older. At this point, then, there are 500 million years of rock missing, and this is very difficult to explain. How could something sit around for one-half billion years and show no signs of erosion, weathering or of catastrophic action?[18]

Geologists do indeed claim that there was erosion taking place at the boundary between the Tapeats Sandstone and the underlying Precambrian rocks before the Tapeats was deposited. On that point the creationists are correct. However, they are entirely incorrect in claiming that geologists say that "all evidences of half billion years of weathering were swept completely away!" Rather, *geologists have documented an abundance of physical evidence which indicates that the boundary is a severe erosional boundary.*

Scientific-creationist literature gives its readers the impression that the Tapeats-Precambrian boundary is a perfectly flat surface with no indication of what Parker called "wavy lines" in the rock. The assumption is that a perfectly horizontal contact would imply virtually continuous deposition. On many individual exposures the contact between Tapeats and the underlying rocks is perfectly horizontal. However, at other exposures and on a *regional* scale the boundary is anything but perfectly horizontal. The complete surface is extremely irregular, indicating that prior to deposition of the Tapeats there was a distinctive, well-established hilly topography.

In some parts of the Grand Canyon, the Tapeats Sandstone overlies the truncated edges of the gently dipping Chuar and Unkar Groups. These groups form a succession of layered sedimentary rocks whose aggregate thickness is about 12,000 feet. Elsewhere the Tapeats directly overlies so-called Archean rocks, including the Vishnu Schist and Zoroaster Granite (figure 3).

The relief * on the unconformable surface beneath the Tapeats is very high. There are places where the uptilted strata of the Shinumo Quartzite penetrate several hundred feet above the general Tapeats-Precambrian surface. The physical evidence indicates that the Shinumo, composed of very tough quartzite, formed erosion-resistant ridges hundreds of feet higher than the plain on which the Tapeats Sandstone was originally deposited. In some locations the ridges of Shinumo are so high that the Bright Angel Shale and not the Tapeats was deposited on top of these Precambrian strata.

A striking example of one of these Precambrian hills can be viewed by tourists from Lipan Point on the south rim of the Canyon. Across the Canyon on its north wall toward the bottom, the angular unconformity between Tapeats and gently eastward tilting Precambrian strata can be plainly seen. The unconformity displays several irregularities and small hills (figure 4).

Besides the ridges of Shinumo, there are also hilly knobs of Archean

---

* *Relief* is a term that indicates the general ruggedness of a terrain. An area of high relief is generally rugged, and one of low relief is generally subdued topography. Specifically, relief is the difference between the point of highest elevation and the point of lowest elevation within the area of interest.

Figure 4. View of the north rim of the Grand Canyon from Lipan Point. The angular unconformity is exposed at the base of the lowest horizontal layer. The unconformity is an erosional surface on the underlying tilted rocks which was later covered by the horizontal layers of Tapeats Sandstone.

granite that penetrate several hundred feet upward into the overlying strata. Locally the Tapeats Sandstone can be seen thinning out against two hills of Archean granite.[19] The relationships are sketched in figure 5. Robert Sharp summarizes the evidence:

> The relief of the . . . surface is controlled by the nature of the underlying rocks, for the highest monadnocks [hills that stand above a surface of erosion] are composed of Shinumo quartzite and massive granite. . . . Hinds (1935, p. 27) reports a maximum relief of 250 feet in the Bright Angel and Vishnu quadrangles, and Noble (1914, p. 51) records a relief of 600 feet in Monadnock Amphitheater in the Shinumo quadrangle. A large monadnock on the north side of the Grand Canyon between Bright Angel and Ninetyone Mile creeks . . . is almost 800 feet high (Wheeler and Kerr, 1936, p. 5), and this is the highest known point on the . . . surface in the Grand Canyon, where more than 95 per cent of the

. . . surface has a relief of less than 150 feet and a large part is essentially flat.[20]

Despite the fact that much of the surface is flat, no one can examine a surface with such extensive relief and justifiably claim that there is no physical evidence for erosion and removal of rock.

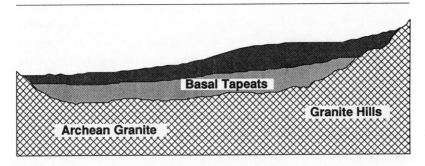

Figure 5. Schematic sketch of the local relationship between the Tapeats Sandstone and underlying Precambrian granite. Modified from Sharp (1941).

In addition to this pronounced irregularity of the surface (what Parker refers to as "wavy lines"), the presence of very thorough weathering of the rock immediately beneath the boundary provides another strong indication that the unconformity represents a previously existing erosional surface along which material was being removed by weathering and erosion. The rocks that are below the unconformity "show extensive weathering to a depth of 10 to 12 feet and in some places are noticeably weathered 50 feet below the surface."[21]

The effects of weathering include chemical breakdown of many of the minerals in the granites and schists beneath the unconformity. In some places there is evidence of a soil zone. Sharp notes that "in places the . . . surface is mantled by a foot or two of structureless, extensively weathered detritus [loose fragments from disintregrating rocks] which passes gradationally upward into the overlying Tapeats and downward into less weathered Archean rock. This layer is considered to be a residual regolith formed by subaerial weathering on the . . . surface."[22]

In still other places the weathered zone is characterized by relatively unweathered residual granite pebbles and boulders derived from the underlying unweathered material embedded in finer, more thoroughly weathered and disintegrated rock. All these features are commonplace in zones of active chemical weathering. And generally where rock is being disintegrated at or below the surface by chemical weathering, that rock is also gradually being removed from the site by erosional processes. In other words, *a weathering rock eventually becomes a "missing" rock.*

Finally, geologists find that much of the reworked weathered material from the soil zone was eventually incorporated into the basal Tapeats Sandstone. "In many localities the basal Tapeats is composed almost entirely of reworked regolith."[23]

Scientific creationists, on the other hand, assert that there is no physical evidence for erosional removal of rock. They are also puzzled that the layered sedimentary rocks of the Chuar and Unkar Groups do not underlie the Tapeats Sandstone everywhere. That the Tapeats Sandstone does not directly overlie the layered rocks everywhere is no problem for geologists. Instead, it is precisely this geometrical arrangement of the rocks that provides one of the premier evidences for an enormous amount of erosion.

Figure 6, which shows the general relationships between the Tapeats and the various Precambrian rocks, indicates just how much rock must have been eroded away. Suppose that the Chuar and Unkar Groups have an average dip of 20 degrees and that their cumulative thickness is about 12,000 feet. The diagram shows that the Chuar and Unkar Groups must have experienced some kind of tilting episode after deposition. Since they are mostly sedimentary rocks, we can assume that they were originally deposited essentially horizontally on the Archean rocks.[24]

But the tilting episode must have occurred prior to deposition of the Tapeats, or the Tapeats would also be tilted. If the Tapeats were

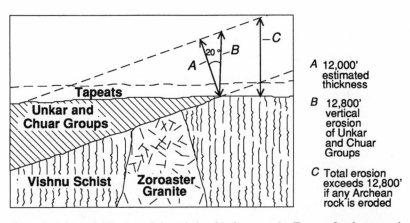

Figure 6. Schematic diagram of the relationship between the Tapeats Sandstone and underlying rocks indicating the amount of erosion that must have taken place prior to the deposition of the Tapeats.

deposited on *both* the Chuar and Unkar Groups *and* the underlying Archean rocks, then a simple trigonometric calculation shows that about 12,800 feet of layered Precambrian sedimentary rocks had to be removed in order for the underlying Archean rocks to be exposed as a land surface and to be covered by the Tapeats.

Moreover, the diagram also shows that some of the Archean also had to be removed. Sharp claims that "the total thickness of rock eroded during the Ep-Algonkian interval is close to 15,000 feet. This is a conservative calculation, and in many places the thicknesses were probably considerably greater."[25]

Clearly there is ample physical evidence pointing to active removal of great thicknesses of rock along the great unconformity. The creationist claim that there is no such evidence is a false assertion made either in ignorance or defiance of a wealth of information available in the professional geological literature.

The Muav-Redwall Contact
A second example of a "missing rock problem" is the boundary between Cambrian and Mississippian strata of the Canyon. It is concern-

ing this boundary that Parker complained of geologists' application of the term *paraconformity* to explain the absence of Ordovician, Silurian and Devonian strata. Burdick also notes:

> As we study the unconformity and paraconformity between the upper formation of the Cambrian Muav limestone and the over-lying formation of the Mississippian Redwall limestone, we wonder why there is supposed to be a gap of some hundred million years in which there is no deposition or erosion. At least none shows up. How can this be? If at present, the rate of erosion is 6.5 inches per 1000 years, at that rate during this time period all the Cambrian formation, and perhaps also the pre-Cambrian formation, should have been eroded. Instead, we find no evidence whatsoever of erosion.[26]

Burdick's claim of "no evidence whatsoever of erosion" is incorrect. Mississippian strata of the canyon are designated as Redwall Lime-stone, owing to the red stain that washes down from the overlying Supai Group over the major cliff about halfway up the canyon. In the Grand Canyon the Redwall is about 500-600 feet thick; south and east of the Canyon the Redwall thins. At Cameron, Arizona, the Redwall is 300 feet thick; near Flagstaff, Arizona, it is about 200 feet thick; and at Holbrook, Arizona, the Redwall has thinned to a negligible thick-ness (figure 7).[27]

In the eastern end of the Grand Canyon, the Redwall Limestone generally rests on top of the Cambrian Muav Limestone, a more thinly-layered, slope-forming unit. In the western end of the Grand Canyon, the Redwall lies above the Devonian Temple Butte Lime-stone which in turn overlies the Muav. Southeast of the Grand Can-yon, the Redwall generally rests on the Devonian Martin Limestone.[28] Because there is ample evidence of Devonian strata beneath the Red-wall, the need is not to account for a Mississippian-Cambrian gap, as claimed by creationists, but to explain the nature of the Mississippian-Devonian boundary. In either case there is ample evidence for ero-sion of material.

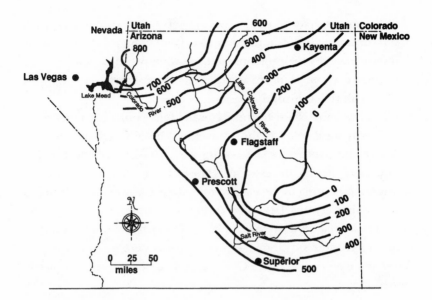

Figure 7. Variations in the total thickness (in feet) of the Redwall Limestone in Arizona. Modified from McKee and Gutschick (1969).

Scientific creationists have stated that where the contact between Redwall and Muav or Temple Butte is exposed there is no obvious evidence of erosion. According to geologists McKee and Gutschick, "At 11 of 21 localities examined, including most of those in eastern Grand Canyon, no evidence of an erosion surface could be detected at the contact: the surface appeared even and flat."[29]

At the other ten localities, however, McKee and Gutschick found evidence for erosion—namely, the presence of shallow channels with minor relief excavated into the upper surface of the Muav or Temple Butte. The channels are typically filled, at least in part, by conglomerate containing angular fragments of chert, limestone or dolomite derived from the underlying Temple Butte or Muav Limestones. McKee and Gutschick concluded that

removal by beveling of a considerable thickness of Devonian strata

in the eastern part of the region may be shown by the great eastward thinning of this formation (the Temple Butte) within a short
distance and by the remnants of once-widespread Devonian strata
preserved in isolated erosion pockets in eastern Grand Canyon
and in Marble Canyon.[30]

Specifically, with regard to the Redwall-Muav contact, a number of
sites display local relief at the contact and basal conglomerate containing some pebbles of underlying rock. But one of the primary
evidences of significant erosion is the very fact that the Devonian
units thin to nothing in the eastern end of the Canyon. Such thinning
implies either (1) that Devonian rocks were not originally deposited
toward that area because that area was somewhat elevated and thus
subject to erosion, or (2) that Devonian rocks were originally deposited in the eastern end of the Canyon area and have been completely
eroded away.

McKee and Gutschick also traced the Redwall Limestone southeast
of the Grand Canyon and examined its contact with underlying rocks.
They concluded that the boundary between the Redwall and underlying rocks is an erosional surface on the basis of several lines of
evidence: (1) several exposures indicate local surfaces of relief as
much as eight feet, (2) the basal Redwall consists of conglomerate
containing fragments of underlying units, (3) in some exposures the
underlying Devonian rocks (Martin Formation) show tilting beneath
the horizontal Redwall, and (4) in some places the Devonian is completely missing and the Redwall directly overlies the Precambrian
Mazatzal quartzite and contains angular fragments of that quartzite
in its basal layers (figure 8).

McKee and Gutschick concluded: "A summary of available data . . .
on the Redwall-Martin (Mississippian-Devonian) contact in the area
south of the Grand Canyon gives abundant evidence of a broad regional disconformity."[31] The Redwall was clearly deposited on top of
an older eroded land surface with broad, gentle topographic irregularities.

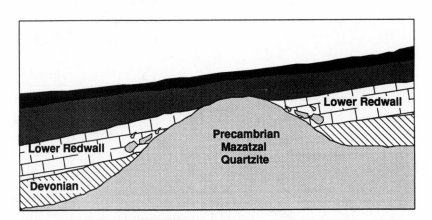

Figure 8. Locally the Redwall Limestone directly overlies Precambrian Mazatzal Quartzite and contains eroded pebbles of the Mazatzal. The quartzite existed as hills throughout early Paleozoic time until deposition of the Redwall around its upper reaches.

Although Ordovician rocks are completely missing from the Grand Canyon, they begin to appear in extreme southeastern Nevada.[32] Moreover, post-Muav Cambrian rocks are found in southeastern Nevada and extreme northwestern Arizona. In other words, the Cambrian, Ordovician and Devonian units thinned drastically eastward toward the Grand Canyon. The Ordovician and Devonian units thinned out completely (figure 9). There are solid grounds for concluding that there are "missing rocks" between the Redwall and Muav, for there are physical evidences of erosion beneath the Redwall, the Devonian units thicken away from the eastern end of the Grand Canyon, and west of the Grand Canyon both Ordovician and Silurian rocks do appear between the Muav and the Devonian Temple Butte.

The Redwall Limestone itself has been subdivided into four distinctive "members," each of which progressively thins toward the southeast. Between each of the members there is also a well-documented erosional surface. Hence there is also "missing rock" within the Mississippian.

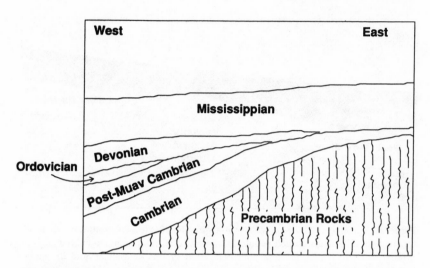

Figure 9. Schematic diagram illustrating the drastic thinning of Lower Paleozoic rocks from west to east in the Grand Canyon area. Note particularly that west of the Grand Canyon, probable Ordovician rocks are present as well as considerable thicknesses of post-Muav Cambrian rocks.

Lastly, Burdick argued that "if six inches per 1000 years erosion is projected, there should be about 50,000 feet of erosion, wiping out all the rocks down to the basement complex. There is no evidence of this."[33] Or, as he put it in a previous quotation, ". . . at that rate during this time period all the Cambrian formation, and perhaps also the pre-Cambrian formation, should have been eroded." Now Burdick has correctly reported the current average rate of erosion within the Colorado Plateau,[34] he has correctly calculated that there should be approximately 50,000 feet of erosion within 100,000,000 years *if* the rate of erosion remained at 6.5 inches per 1000 years, and he has correctly observed that all the Cambrian rocks should have been eroded away at this rate.

But Burdick's overall argument is fallacious because there is no warrant for extrapolating the present high rate of erosion into the past. Certainly no appeal to a principle of uniformity carries with it the requirement that such a rate be extrapolated indefinitely into the past. The plateau is currently at a much higher overall elevation than it was during most of its past, and therefore overall erosion rates are now much higher than they would have been when the plateau was much closer to sea level. The fact that the channels excavated into the Muav are relatively small ones is an indication that the Muav-Temple Butte land surface was not very far above sea level and would therefore not be subject to a high erosion rate.

Furthermore, much of the current high rate of erosion of the plateau is due to the rapid removal of the very soft, easily erodible shales of Cretaceous age (for example, Mancos Shale) that are exposed at the surface. But the limestones of the plateau erode far more slowly than do shales, as indicated by their general tendency to form cliffs and far steeper slopes than the shales. As a result, erosion of the Muav Limestone surface would be expected to be far slower than erosion of soft shales. There is no reason to expect that the erosion rate before deposition of the Redwall was 6.5 inches per 1000 years. There is therefore no reason to expect that 50,000 feet of rock had to be eroded away as Burdick suggests. On the contrary, there is strong reason to expect that erosion rates just prior to Redwall deposition were considerably lower than they are at present, so that no very great thickness of rock had to be eroded away.

The Redwall-Supai Contact

According to scientific creationists, there is also a "problem" of supposedly "missing rock" between the Redwall Limestone and the overlying Supai Group.

Now begins the "missing rock" problem—if we follow the geologic column of the evolutionist. The Pennsylvanian formation, which ought to consume about 50 million years, is missing between the Supai and Mississippian formations. Much of the Mississippian is also missing. Generally the explanation given by evolutionists is that a mountain stood above water for a long time and, thus, there are no deposits of Pennsylvanian. In that case there ought to be signs of erosion. Nothing can just stand still for 50 million years and show no evidence. And we do find the Pennsylvanian in the Colorado plateau country and in the San Juan area of southeast Utah. From an evolutionist viewpoint it is difficult to explain the absence of the Pennsylvanian and of much of the Mississippian.[35] But once again, the mystery of the "missing rock" is no more than an artifact of misinformation and misleading argumentation.

The Redwall Limestone is overlain by the Supai Group, formerly designated the Supai Formation. The Supai Group, recently so designated by McKee, consists of four formations, the three lowest of which are Pennsylvanian in age, and the uppermost of which, the Esplanade Sandstone, is Permian.[36] Thus to claim that the Pennsylvanian System is missing from the Grand Canyon is incorrect. Some Pennsylvanian material is undoubtedly missing, but this cannot be said of the entire Pennsylvanian System. It can further be shown that some of the lower Supai formations are approximately correlative with the Pennsylvanian strata of southeastern Utah.

Scientific creationists have implied that there are no signs of erosion between the Redwall and the Supai: "Nothing can just stand still for 50 million years and show no evidence." At first glance it might appear to the casual observer that there are no signs of erosion. McKee and Gutschick stated: "Despite the magnitude of the stratigraphic break represented, the contact between the Redwall Limestone and the Supai Formation as viewed *from a distance* (emphasis ours) appears remarkably even and in most places gives little suggestion of the presence of any important unconformity. Strata of the two formations are nearly everywhere similar in attitude, and in most places rapid weathering of weak beds immediately above the Redwall Limestone has caused its upper contact to be concealed by talus."[37] *But despite this initial superficial appearance of a lack of erosion, there is a wealth of evidence along the Redwall-Supai boundary to indicate that intense erosion and weathering have taken place.*

The lowermost formation of the Supai Group is called the Watahomigi Formation. McKee has documented numerous large scours and channels that were excavated into the upper surface of the Redwall, subsequently filled in by pre-Watahomigi sediments, and then completely covered by Watahomigi sediments.[38] McKee's monumental publication on the Supai Group even includes an entire chapter on "Pre-Supai Buried Valleys." According to McKee

> these valleys average about 1000 feet in width and 280 feet in depth with a maximum depth of 401 feet. . . . Apparently the valleys are parts of an extensive drainage system formed after Redwall deposition had ceased; they were completely filled with sediment, partly marine and partly continental by the close of Late Mississippian (Chesterian) time.[39]

McKee's monograph includes several excellent photographs of these buried valleys. McKee concluded, on the basis of the existence of these valleys, that "the area must have been uplifted more than 400 ft above sea level . . . to have permitted dissection to that depth."[40] Because streams are not capable of eroding significantly below sea level, running water could not have scoured a 400-foot-deep channel into the Redwall surface unless the land had been elevated at least 400 feet above sea level.

Evidence for erosion is indicated not only by these deep channels but also by conglomerate deposits at the base of the Watahomigi Formation and in the bottom of the channel fills. The pebbles in the basal conglomerates of the Watahomigi are generally composed of chert (a hard, dense, compact rock, commonly layered, that is composed of very fine, crystalline silica), but other rock types may be present. Nearly all pebbles are of very resistant rock types. McKee comments,

> Evidence that the basal Watahomigi conglomerates were derived from a relatively close source is the comparatively small amount of rounding on most pebbles. Surfaces characteristic of strong attrition through rolling by wave action are absent on most specimens;

the dominantly chert composition may be attributed to derivation from the underlying Redwall Limestone of Mississippian age.[41] The Redwall does contain thin layers and nodules of chert, and during the weathering of the underlying Redwall, the relatively chemically resistant chert would survive the weathering process much more easily than the more readily destructible limestone.

But there is more. The upper part of the Redwall is also characterized by many cavities and depressions that are commonly filled with limestone breccia (rock composed of large angular fragments of limestone cemented together) or with distorted fine-grained red sediments that have clearly been derived from the overlying Supai. These features are indicative of the development of karst topography on the upper surface of the Redwall prior to Supai deposition.

Karst, an area of eroded limestone, is a characteristic topography in locations that are underlain by limestone layers, as found in large parts of Florida, Illinois or Kentucky. In such regions the limestone dissolves in circulating ground water, thus forming large crevices and even caverns. The roof rock may collapse into the caves or crevices so that the cavities become filled with fragmented limestone blocks or loose sediments that may have overlain the limestone. Sinkholes, that is, circular surface depressions, may develop if the effects of collapse reach the surface.

Now, the upper surface of the Redwall Limestone displays these characteristic karst features. This evidence further points to an extended period of weathering and erosion on an exposed Redwall land surface prior to deposition of the Supai. After resubmergence of the weathered and eroded Redwall surface, the Supai (Watahomigi) was deposited and its red muds were washed down into the cavities in the underlying Redwall.

Thus to claim that there is no physical evidence for an erosional break between the Mississippian and the Supai is to fly in the face of a wealth of fully documented geological data. The scientific-creationist claim for a lack of erosion can be made only if one is willing to ignore the total regional relationships between superposed units. The claim can be made only on the bases of examinations from a long distance across the Canyon where there is a superficial appearance of conformity and of close inspection of some exposures where there is local conformity. As soon as one considers the regional picture and all available exposures of the boundary, it becomes clear that there is abundant evidence of erosion between the Redwall and the Supai.

The scientific creationists have also neglected to mention that there are similar compelling evidences of erosional episodes recorded by several unconformities within the Supai Group. There is, for example, a prominent erosional surface between each of the four formations of the Supai Group. Still further, there is also an important erosional surface within the Watahomigi Formation. For more detail on these thoroughly documented erosional surfaces, the reader is invited to consult the chapter, "Erosion Surfaces," in McKee's professional paper.[42]

Mesozoic and Cenozoic Rocks

Scientific creationists have also claimed that there is a problem with standard geology because of the suggestion that the entire Mesozoic and Cenozoic sections are "missing" from the Grand Canyon. It is not clear why the absence of these rocks should pose a problem for geologists. In this case, even scientific creationists must admit the "missing rock" once existed. There is no need to establish its former existence by pointing out evidences of previous erosion along unconformities as with, say, the Redwall-Supai boundary. One simply cannot claim that geologists have invented the idea of "missing rock" in this case. The reason is, as even scientific creationists have recognized, that thick Mesozoic and Cenozoic layers are present all over the Colorado Plateau. A thick Mesozoic section exists immediately to the north and east of the Canyon toward Vermilion and Echo Cliffs. It is evident to any thoughtful observer that the Mesozoic rocks, exposed all around the base of the Kaibab-Coconino uplift through which the

Canyon has been excavated, have been eroded from the top of this uplift.

Much of the Colorado Plateau northeast of the Grand Canyon contains spectacular exposures of Triassic, Jurassic, Cretaceous and Tertiary layers that are unquestionably superimposed stratigraphically on top of the layers exposed at the Grand Canyon. For example, the Triassic Moenkopi, Chinle and Wingate Formations are beautifully displayed at Capitol Reef National Park in south-central Utah, as well as just north and east of the Grand Canyon. The Jurassic Navajo Sandstone is 2000 feet thick at Zion National Park in southwestern Utah, as well as at Vermilion Cliffs just north of the Canyon. An 800-foot thickness of the Jurassic Entrada Sandstone can be seen resting on top of the Navajo Sandstone at Arches National Park. The Jurassic Morrison Formation occurs at Dinosaur National Monument on the Colorado-Utah boundary, as well as 150 miles east of the Grand Canyon. The Cretaceous Mancos and Mesa Verde Formations that overlie the Morrison and Dakota Formations are easily seen in the Book Cliffs of northern Utah and at Mesa Verde National Park in southwestern Colorado. The Tertiary Wasatch and Green River Formations can be seen lying on top of the Mesa Verde in western Colorado and northern Utah. Yet all these great thicknesses of rock are missing in the Grand Canyon area, owing in large part to removal by erosion from above the layers of rock that are now present at the Canyon.

Evaluation of the Scientific-Creationist Argument

We have examined in some detail one of the major scientific-creationist assertions about the Grand Canyon, namely, that there is no evidence for any significant erosion of rock prior to deposition of the overlying layer. The claim is that there exists no basis for the geologists' talk about "missing layers of rock." It has been shown, however, that this scientific-creationist claim is without foundation and is discredited by a diverse array of abundant physical evidence found in the Grand Canyon region. Similarly, the other major claims made by scientific creationists about the Grand Canyon can also be shown to be in error.

A number of important conclusions can be drawn about the scientific-creationist reasoning through this analysis of a claim that typifies the scientific-creationist approach to geology:

1. *Major distinctive scientific-creationist claims about geology betray a glaring lack of familiarity with relevant professional literature.* This lack of familiarity leads to a failure to engage in the critical discussion of data relevant to the claims being made, to misstatement of basic data and to misunderstanding of basic principles of geology. Regarding the specific claim that there is no evidence of erosion between layers in the Grand Canyon, the writings of Lang, Burdick and other scientific creationists are devoid of documentation which could have provided important geological data about the Canyon. In vain one looks for references to technical geological literature on the Canyon and its environs. Surely those anxious to propose the flood as an alternative theory for the geology ought to appeal to technical literature for relevant observations that would have to be accounted for more satisfactorily by a catastrophic flood.

Scientific creationists have as much right as anyone to construct a theory of the geological history of the Canyon. If, however, they expect their theory to receive serious consideration in the geological community, they must deal with the data that have already been collected by trained professionals. Scientific creationism will not be taken seriously as science if "flood geologists" are content to make sweeping generalizations based solely on a few disconnected observations. Scientific creationists must be prepared to explain in detail how their flood model accounts for channel fills, for pebbles within those channel fills, for karst features such as caverns and sinkholes, for weathering and fossil soil zones beneath unconformities, for the existence of angular discordance beneath some unconformities and for the presence of several unconformities within the Canyon and throughout the entire Colorado Plateau. If scientific creationists wish to have their theories taken seriously, they must discontinue their current practice of ignoring the professional geological literature that discusses the observation of these critically important details.

The general lack of awareness of professional geological literature has resulted in repeated misstatement of fundamental information in scientific-creationist writings. For example, Burdick, Lang and other writers have built a case around the lack of Pennsylvanian rocks in the Grand Canyon while laboring under the mistaken impressions that the Supai is entirely Permian and that the Pennsylvanian System is completely missing from the Grand Canyon. Acquaintance with the technical literature could have prevented those mistakes. Much of the Supai in the Canyon is generally regarded by geologists as Pennsylvanian.

Another misstatement of fact is the assertion that geologists claim the Canyon to be "a prime example of the geologic column for in the Canyon more strata of the column are found than anywhere else in the world."[43] This misstatement then serves as the basis for an argument against standard geology for "more than one-half the strata are missing in the Canyon."[44]

The first quotation is blatantly in error. No geologist would ever claim that the Canyon has more strata of the geologic column than anywhere else in the world for the simple reason that any geologist who knows the Grand Canyon knows that the Ordovician and Silurian are entirely missing and that significant portions of the Devonian and Mississippian are also lacking. Geologists also know that no Triassic, Jurassic, Cretaceous or Tertiary strata are present in the walls of the Canyon.

Any North American geologist would agree that the Appalachians provide a more complete representation of the column than does the Grand Canyon. In the Valley and Ridge province of the Appalachians in eastern Pennsylvania there are as much as 40,000 feet of Paleozoic rocks exposed, including Cambrian, Ordovician, Silurian, Devonian, Mississippian and Pennsylvanian, but no Permian rocks. There are only about 4500 feet of Paleozoic rocks at the Grand Canyon. The Canyon provides an outstanding example of geology because the rocks are so well exposed and are relatively undeformed compared with the Appalachians, but the rock record in the Grand Canyon is much less complete.

Lack of familiarity with the literature has led also to a misunderstanding of basic geological concepts. Scientific creationists persistently misunderstand the principle of uniformity. There is among scientific creationists the impression that, on the basis of uniformity, geologists do or must extrapolate all presently measurable rates backward in time indefinitely. Hence Burdick bases an argument against missing rock on the mistaken assumption that the Colorado Plateau region has experienced a rate of erosion of 6.5 inches per 1000 years throughout its entire history. There seems to be no awareness by scientific creationists that geologists recognize that rates of many processes can vary drastically through time depending on material conditions and that such variation is not in conflict with a principle of uniformity.[45]

Similarly, scientific creationists do not appear to understand the basic concept of the geologic column. They have created the impression that orthodox geology has severe difficulties with the Grand Canyon because of its acceptance of "the geologic column." Scientific creationists seem to think that geologists pretend that all the systems of the geologic column are, or should be, represented by actual rock in continuous successions of layers all over the world. Thus, if scientific creationists could show that real rock successions are lacking representatives of some of the geologic systems, the inference to be drawn is that the concept of the geologic column is severely deficient.

This view, however, completely misrepresents what geologists say about the column. The geologic column is an *idealized* composite constructed from real rock successions around the world on the basis of the principle of superposition.[46] Every geologist knows that some systems are going to be missing from any real rock succession for the simple reason that sedimentation has not occurred and should not be expected to occur continuously through time at any one place on the face of the earth. There is no reason to expect that a sedimentary basin will remain a basin permanently. Geologists would, in fact, be very much surprised to find an area in which the geologic column was completely represented, for that would imply that the area had remained a basin of deposition throughout the whole of geologic time until extremely recently when it was uplifted, eroded and exposed to view.

Once a basin is uplifted, erosion will begin to remove sediment or rock that has already accumulated in the basin. No new sediment or rock will be deposited until the uplift has been worn down by erosion and is once more depressed to form a basin. For example, a basin that had accumulated sediments through Cambrian, Ordovician and Silurian time may be uplifted during Devonian time and may once again subside in Mississippian time. The result will be that during Devonian time, some and maybe all of the Silurian sediments will be eroded away. If all the Silurian layers are eroded away, then some and maybe all of the underlying Ordovician rocks will be eroded away. If all the Ordovician layers are eroded away, then some and maybe all of the underlying Cambrian rocks will be eroded away. And so on.

The amount of erosion that takes place will depend on many factors such as climate, severity of the uplift and composition of the rocks being eroded. The more severe the uplift, the more likely it is that a lot of rock will be eroded. Moreover, during Devonian time, since erosion is occurring, no Devonian sediments will be deposited. Once the basin forms again in Mississippian time, then Mississippian sediments will be deposited, but they will rest on top of either Silurian, Ordovician or Cambrian deposits, and there will be some kind of unconformity between the Mississippian and underlying rocks. This is exactly what we see in the Grand Canyon beneath the Redwall Limestone.

Many places on the continental land surfaces are not now receiving any permanent accumulation of sediments. Thus the present time period will not be represented by rocks of the present in those places in the future. Therefore, it is no surprise whatsoever to a geologist that some systems are missing from the Grand Canyon area or anywhere else. During the development of the stratigraphy of the Grand Canyon there were times when the area was somewhat above sea level, thus not receiving sediments, and was experiencing mild erosion of previously deposited rocks. For example, at present, the area is well above sea level, is receiving little new sediment and is experiencing intense erosion. Rocks of the present will not be represented in the Grand Canyon of the future!

2. *The flood model entails a lack of external consistency with relevant bodies of knowledge.* This point could be developed at great length by considering the fact that the various scientific-creationist claims about the Grand Canyon are totally incompatible with the established results of radiometric dating and biogeography.[47] On these grounds alone the global flood theory is strongly suspect. This lack of external consistency is exemplified by the failure of scientific creationists to consider *regional* geology in their theorizing.

For example, scientific-creationist claims about a lack of erosion in the layers of the Grand Canyon are made on the basis of casual observations of rock exposures along the major hiking trails. A case is then built on a few isolated observations abstracted from the larger, regional context of the layers. One cannot argue from a few exposures of the Redwall-Supai boundary showing no evident signs of erosion that there is no erosion at the Redwall-Supai boundary. The geologist must consider that boundary on a regional scale, and that requires examination of dozens of exposures at widely separated areas as well as any available information from well drilling that would shed light on the regional relationships between rock units.

Similarly one cannot argue for continuous deposition of Redwall on top of Muav only on the basis of what can be seen in one part of the Grand Canyon. The geologist must also consider the regional geology which indicates that west of the Grand Canyon several formations begin to wedge in between the Muav and the Redwall. Scientific creationists could have avoided mistakes about the Redwall Limestone if they had learned about its regional relationships and distribution, and had not been content to confine their studies to only a few isolated occurrences within the tourist part of the Canyon. It is small wonder that geologists will not take scientific-creationist theorizing seriously when it fails to reckon with basic, relevant bodies of information and seeks instead to develop theories that are inconsistent with that information.

3. *The flood model lacks internal coherence.* Scientific creationists have claimed that between layers of rock in the Grand Canyon there is no evidence for erosion at all and that the layers were deposited successively and continuously by great flood waves passing back and forth across the face of the earth. But if the flood model is correct, then there should be abundant signs of erosion between layers, especially if those layers were still soft and unconsolidated as most flood geologists believe! Indeed, flood geologists repeatedly talk of the tremendous erosive capabilities of the flood.

Suppose that a thick layer of soft mud, just deposited from a great flood wave passing to the east, is briefly exposed to the air. Another gigantic wave comes surging back from the opposite direction. The wave is charged with suspended sediment eroded from highlands to the east. That such a turbulent wave loaded with sediment should pass over the soft mud without in the least disturbing its upper surface is not even remotely credible. There would unquestionably be severe scouring and churning of the mud. The supposed absence of erosion between layers to which scientific creationists appeal would be a strong argument *against* a global flood that consisted of a succession of waves!

4. *The flood model lacks predictive accuracy.* Scientific creationists claim that the Tapeats-Precambrian boundary represents the onset of the flood and that the other layer boundaries are not erosional but rep-

resent essentially continuous sedimentation from sweeping flood waves. If the preflood land surface is identified with the great unconformity at the base of the Tapeats Sandstone, then this land surface should have had vegetation growing all over it. Moreover, that land surface should have had a variety of animals living on it, animals originally created by God only a few thousands of years earlier. That land surface should have had turtles, snakes, small mammals in burrows like gophers and ground hogs, crocodiles, freshwater fish living in streams. Once the flood came, all of these life forms should have been overwhelmed and suddenly buried in the mass of sediment that became the Tapeats Sandstone. The flood model should predict the occurrence of a wide variety of fossils in the Tapeats, but they are not there. Where are the fossil turtles, snakes, trees, bushes, grasses, mice, ground hogs, lizards and sloths in the Tapeats? They have never been found.

If the formations above the Tapeats were deposited virtually continuously by successive flood waves, then we should expect to find certain kinds of fossil organisms. If a flood wave that deposited the Redwall Limestone had swept into the area from an adjacent land mass, then we would have expected to find a host of vegetation and land animals. Instead we find only marine fossils. But if the flood wave swept out of the ocean, why is the Redwall *totally* lacking in such marine forms as whales, seals, walruses, dolphins, sea birds, ichthyosaurs, all kinds of fish and sea snakes? Moreover, if these animals were buried rapidly, we should expect to find whole skeletons. We don't even find individual vertebrae.

If a flood wave that deposited the Supai swept into the area from a continental highland nearby, then why, as with the Tapeats, do we find absolutely no signs of trees or shrubs, shrews, frogs and a host of other land animals that could not possibly escape to higher ground? The Supai contains only a limited selection of fossil amphibians and reptiles. Why are there no mammals, trees or shrubs? The flood model utterly fails to predict the observed paleontology of the

Grand Canyon formations with even the slightest degree of accuracy.

Conclusion

If space permitted, analysis of the other claims of scientific creationists about the Grand Canyon would repeatedly indicate their lack of familiarity with the relevant literature. By its failure to deal with a wealth of relevant data, the recent creation-global flood model is unable to display the appropriate characteristics of a credible scientific theory such as external consistency, internal coherence, predictive ability and ability to account for a wide diversity of geological phenomena. Scientific creationists cannot expect geologists to take flood theories seriously until such theories demonstrate the appropriate characteristics. And that will not happen unless scientific creationists become sufficiently familiar with geological observations that have been made by trained professionals and demonstrate that they can treat those observations competently and with professional integrity.

SCIENCE HELD HOSTAGE BY NATURALISM PART III

Earlier in this book we carefully delineated the domain of natural science. By agreeing to limit its attention to an empirically based study of the intelligibility of the physical world, natural science has chosen to maintain a respectful silence on questions regarding the relationship of the physical universe to transcendent beings or powers. In this way persons representing a broad diversity of religious perspectives can fruitfully work together within the scientific community.

However, perhaps because of the respect and credibility that the sciences have rightfully gained, many persons have been tempted to exploit the good name of science by speaking as if their particular religious or ideological perspective were derivable solely from the established results of scientific investigation.

In this final part we call attention to the way in which the ideology of naturalism has failed to honor the limitations of natural science and has sought instead to hold science hostage to support the tenets of its own form of religious faith.

POPULAR PORTRAITS OF SCIENCE: FOCUSED OR FUZZY?

7

I N CHAPTER ONE WE POINTED OUT THAT THE DO-main of the natural sciences is restricted to questions regarding the physical properties, patterns of behavior and formative history of the physical universe. We argued that questions concerning the governance of the physical behavior or formative history of the universe, or questions about the relationship of the physical universe to transcendent or nonmaterial beings, such as God or angels, lie outside of the scientific domain. Such questions must be answered, not on scientific, but on religious or philosophical grounds. Because of such considerations, we would maintain that the domain of natural science is not being respected by those Christians, however well-meaning, who assert that the concepts of divine creation and providence are derivable from the discoveries of science. On the other hand, and with equal insistence, we maintain that the proponents of philosophical naturalism also fail to respect the domain of natural science when they assert that it is from the results of natural science that they reach their conclusions that there is no God, or that the universe is self-existent, self-contained and self-governing.

In reality, much of today's popular scientific writing adopts neither an explicitly Christian nor an explicitly naturalistic stance. A Christian position is not commonly expressed in the popular scientific writings of professional, practicing scientists.[1] But neither is the blatant philosophical naturalism of such writers as Carl Sagan or P. W. Atkins commonplace in popular scientific writing.[2] Much of the scientific writing for the general public today is done in such a manner that the domain and limitations of natural science are reasonably well recognized. As a result, the writers do not appear to be trying to sharpen any religious or philosophical ax on a scientific grindstone, and the reader may often be hard-pressed to discover very much about the religious or philosophical leanings of the authors.

Contrary to a common impression among evangelical Christians that scientists are hostile to religious belief, we discover that much current writing does not attempt to make religious claims on scientific grounds. For example, many recent books written in defense of organic evolution and in opposition to scientific creationism are commendable for their careful avoidance of using natural science as a tool to attack religious belief.[3] The domain of science is generally understood and respected. Among the better books to appear are Norman D. Newell's *Creation and Evolution,* Niles Eldredge's *The Monkey Business,* Michael Ruse's *Darwinism Defended* and Philip Kitcher's *Abusing Science.*[4]

All of these works explicitly discuss, or incidentally touch on, the proper domain of science. They recognize that discussions about God, providence or ethics are, by their very nature, not scientific discussions, because their subject matter lies outside the province of natural science. None of these writers makes any explicit claim to belief in God. Nor do they openly commit themselves to any religious position. But neither do any of them reject the legitimacy of belief in God or the compatibility of such belief with a scientific investigation of the universe. Even while vigorously defending biological evolution, these authors stress that biological evolution is not antithetical to the idea of God. And while not necessarily committed to it themselves, they all recognize the legitimacy of some form of theistic perspective on evolution.

These four writers seem to be open to the compatibility of science and religion. If there is fault to be found, it is perhaps that they appear to consider science and religion as so remotely different from one another that conflict would necessarily be out of the question because the fundamental concerns of religion and science are unrelated. They are often considered virtually separate compartments of life. Eldredge, for example, is critical of the fundamentalist perception that science and religion are in conflict. But this need not be, says Eldredge, for "science seeks to understand the universe in naturalistic terms. It depends upon observation, accepts nothing on faith and acknowledges that it can never claim to know the ultimate truth,"[5] and between religion and science, "most scientists and members of religious communities see no conflict, as the two systems are completely different, are pursued for different reasons and serve different functions."[6]

Seeing basic distinctions, many recent defenders of biological evolution also understand the limits of natural science well enough to recognize that standards of right and wrong are not to be derived from scientific theory. None of the four writers noted is guilty of adopting evolutionary ethics. They are as critical of social Darwinism as any scientific creationist.[7] These authors do not fall into the trap of attempting to derive ethical principles from scientific theories. Philip Kitcher, for example, claims that "what is evolutionarily useful, or even necessary, may not be morally correct.[8]

While recognizing that much popular scientific literature does an acceptable job of respecting the limits of science by not making unwarranted assertions about religion or ethics in the name of science, two books will now be considered briefly that *do* overstep the proper bounds of science. On the one hand is Isaac Asimov's book *In the Beginning;*[9] on the other is Douglas Futuyma's *Science on Trial.*[10] Asimov's book is an example of naive scientism at its worst.[11] Although not obviously operating from a position of overt philosophical naturalism, Asimov does try to draw deistic or agnostic religious conclusions from scientific discovery. Futuyma's book, in many respects an excellent work and far more worthwhile than Asimov's, contains much more subtle examples of the failure to respect the boundary of the proper domain of natural science.

Asimov's *In the Beginning* is a verse-by-verse scientific and religious commentary on the first eleven chapters of Genesis.[12] In some ways this book is a counterpart of Henry Morris's *The Genesis Record,*[13] although Morris's commentary deals with the entire book of Genesis. While Morris writes as one unashamedly devoted to Scripture as the Word of God, Asimov nowhere makes any commitment to Scripture as being anything more than a fascinating religious book.[14] And while Morris takes pains to show how Scripture, interpreted in his literalistic manner, completely agrees with the "true facts of science" as understood by scientific creationism, Asimov constantly seeks to show that Scripture, as interpreted according to the documentary hypothesis, presents points of view that are radically different from those that he considers to be deducible from the scientific world-picture.

In this book, Asimov does not explicitly discuss the domain and limitations of science. His comments, however, do strongly suggest that he believes that science is able to establish certain metaphysical parameters about the ultimate character of reality. For example, he notes that the Bible presents a sophisticated picture of a monotheistic god who "constantly engages himself in the minutiae of his creation."[15] But in contrast to the biblical view, Asimov believes that over the past four centuries,

> scientists have built up an alternate picture of the Universe. . . . The
> natural phenomena of Earth and of the Universe have seemed to
> fall into place bit by bit as behavior that is random, spontaneous,
> unwilled, and that takes place within the constraints of the "laws
> of nature." Scientists grew increasingly reluctant to suppose that
> the workings of the laws of nature were ever interfered with. . . .
> Certainly, no such interference was ever observed, and the tales of
> such interferences in the past came to seem increasingly dubious.
>
> In short, the scientific view sees the Universe as following its own
> rules blindly, without either interference or direction.[16]

Here Asimov has given a misleading impression of the scientific approach to the study of the world. Some individual scientists may have
reached the conclusion that natural behavior is blind and unwilled
by anything outside nature. However, science as a professional, communal enterprise has never made any judgment that natural behavior
is either blind and unwilled or directed and willed by something
outside of nature. Furthermore, science has made no judgment as to
whether or not "interferences" with the supposed "laws of nature" are
possible or have happened.[17] Because science functions without making judgments about such matters as external direction, interference
or will, it may appear to the casual observer that science describes the
universe *as if* the forces of the universe and the "laws of nature" were
unwilled, blind and undirected. Such an observation, however, is very
different from the claim that science has made the judgment that the
behavior of the universe *is* in actuality unwilled, undirected and blind.

Furthermore, Asimov steps completely beyond the bounds of
science without being candid about what he is doing. On the basis of
scientific method he claims to draw a variety of metaphysical conclusions. He continues,

> That still leaves it possible that God created the Universe to begin
> with and designed the laws of nature that govern its behavior. From
> this standpoint, the Universe might be viewed as a wind-up toy,

which God has wound up once and for all and which is now winding down and working itself out in all its intricacy without having to be touched at all.

If so, that reduces God's involvement to a minimum and makes one wonder if he is needed at all. . . .

So far, scientists have not uncovered any evidence that would hint that the workings of the Universe require the action of a divine being. On the other hand, scientists have uncovered no evidence that indicates that a divine being does *not* exist.[18]

This quotation is replete with what we consider to be intolerable assertions. In the first place Asimov is guilty of the common error of thinking that the "laws of nature" govern the behavior of the universe. They do no such thing. As pointed out in chapter one, the "laws of nature" are only our finite and fallible attempts at describing the regular patterns of behavior that we observe in the world around us. The identity of the ultimate power that governs those patterns must be determined on extra-scientific grounds.

Additionally, it appears that Asimov thinks of natural science as such a comprehensive method of discovering knowledge that it is within the capability of science to uncover, recognize, evaluate and interpret evidence for or against the existence of God. Not only so, but Asimov speaks as if science can potentially decide the relationship of whatever god there may be to the universe. Science, in his view, ultimately has the power to determine whether or not a theistic, deistic or atheistic world view is legitimate. He continues to make the totally unwarranted assumption that, since science is able to describe the intrinsic intelligibility of the universe without reference to the agency of external spiritual beings, therefore the universe in fact operates solely in terms of purely blind, impersonal law. It seems not to have occurred to Asimov that God may act immanently within the universe in such a manner that we perceive that matter and energy behave in regular and usefully predictable patterns.

Contrary to Asimov's assertions, however, professional natural science can make no judgments as to whether or not we live in a theistic, deistic or atheistic universe. Such conclusions are entirely beyond the capabilities of science with its methods of empirical observation and testing. We regret that such a widely read popularizer as Asimov has not been more careful in giving proper guidance to the general public on such an important matter as the limitations of natural science with respect to religion and philosophy. Sadly he has not honored the proper domain and boundaries of science. He has incorrectly transposed the *methodological* naturalism of professional natural science into a universal *ontological* or *metaphysical* naturalism. By his failure to honor the boundaries of the scientific domain, Asimov gives religiously sensitive persons a bad impression of natural science, making it appear as the opponent of any theistic perspective. Irresponsible rhetoric of this sort provides much of the fuel for the creation-evolution debate.

Next we consider Douglas Futuyma's book *Science on Trial*. The general reader would do far better to read Futuyma than Asimov. Futuyma is a totally convinced evolutionist, and he defends the neo-Darwinian theory of evolution with enthusiasm and ability.[19] Contrary to what many Christians might expect about those who accept evolution, Futuyma, although certainly not claiming to be a theistic evolutionist, does not promote naturalistic evolutionism.

To Futuyma, biological evolution is a scientific theory only and is not a comprehensive explanation for the totality of existence. As a careful scholar who respects the boundaries of science, he further recognizes, unlike Asimov, that many questions that people ask are of a philosophical, religious, ethical or aesthetic nature and cannot fruitfully be addressed or answered by natural science. Thus, for example, Futuyma, like Ruse, does not draw his ethics from the biological theory of natural selection. He takes great pains to reject social Darwinism and so-called evolutionary ethics. Indeed, he speaks of social Darwinism as a "perversion of biology"[20] and also states "Nor is there any moral imperative in evolution telling us that we ought to progress, nor any deity called Natural Selection telling us that we ought to compete. Natural selection may be a 'law of nature;' but a scientific law, like the 'law of gravity,' is merely a description of a regularity in natural processes, not a rule of conduct."[21]

The following extended selections from Futuyma's work contrast very favorably with the quotation from Asimov and show that Futuyma understands what science can and cannot do. For example,

> it is important to recognize that not all "facts" are susceptible to scientific investigation, simply because some observations and experiences are entirely personal. I cannot prove that someone loves his or her child. The emotions that any individual claims to have are not susceptible to scientific documentation, because they cannot be independently verified by other observers. In other words, science seeks to explain only objective knowledge, knowledge that can be acquired independently by different investigators if they follow a prescribed course of observation or experiment.
>
> Many human experiences and concerns are not objective, and so do not fall within the realm of science. As a result, science has nothing to say about aesthetics or morality. It cannot provide an objective basis on which to judge whether or not Beethoven wrote great music, or whether or not an act is ethical. The functioning of human society, then, clearly requires principles that stem from some source other than science. While science can provide objective knowledge, we must look elsewhere for guidance on how to use that knowledge.[22]

Futuyma also recognizes that science as such cannot develop explanations about God and his relationship to the world:

> Any "theory" that explains phenomena by recourse to the actions of an omnipotent, omniscient supreme being, or any other supernatural omnipotent entity, is a nonscientific theory. I could postulate that all human actions are slavish responses to the suggestions of guardian angels and diabolical incubi, and no one could possibly prove me wrong; for whether a person's actions look rational

or irrational, good or evil, I can involve the power of supernatural suggestion. I could similarly postulate that God personally has governed the development and life of every creature that has ever been born, and if you protest that the laws of physics, chemistry, and biology explain biological phenomena, I could answer that God in his wisdom sees fit to act in an orderly way that gives the appearance of material laws of causation.

Because such a theory cannot be challenged by any observation, it is not scientific. It isn't necessarily wrong. It is just not amenable to scientific investigation. Science cannot deny the existence of supernatural beings. It cannot prove that God didn't create the universe. . . . Science can neither affirm nor deny supernatural powers. Science is the exercise of reason, and so is limited to questions that can be approached by the use of reason, questions that can be answered by the discovery of objective knowledge and the elucidation of natural laws of causation. In dealing with questions about the natural world, scientists must act as if they can be answered without recourse to supernatural powers. There can be no scientific study of God.[23]

So far, so good. Futuyma has done a commendable job in paying careful attention to the bounds of scientific investigation and in recognizing that science cannot be used to draw conclusions about the relationship of God to the world. Futuyma is not guilty of espousing naturalism or materialism in the name of science. But now we issue a caution. Despite Futuyma's recognition of and respect for the limits of science, he does make a number of assertions that are phrased in such a way that an undiscerning reader may be strongly inclined to draw metaphysical conclusions from science. Below we discuss four examples of such unfortunate language.

1. The mind that cannot abide uncertainty is troubled by the idea that the human species developed by "chance." But whether we evolved by chance or not depends on what the word means. We did not arise by a fortuitous aggregation of molecules, but rather

by a nonrandom process—natural selection favoring some genes over others. But we are indeed a product of chance in that we were not predestined, from the beginning of the world, to come into existence. Like the extinction of the dodo, the death of Rosencrantz and Guildenstern, or the outbreak of World War I, we are a product of a history that might have been different.[24]

It is not clear whether or not Futuyma is making a metaphysical assertion here. He might simply be claiming that, just as humans cannot predict the outcome of history, so, too, we could not have predicted the certain appearance of the human race. In other words, *from a purely biological perspective,* human beings were not predestined to appear. If that is all that Futuyma means, then there is little cause for disagreement. On the other hand, if Futuyma is making a metaphysical assertion, then he ought to have identified it as such and also indicated that such an assertion could not be made on the basis of science.

Christians, of course, confess that God is sovereign over history from beginning to end, and that the human race is not just an afterthought in the mind of God but was specifically brought into the world as the crown of creation. In the Christian world view, human beings most certainly were predestined, *from a theological perspective,* from the beginning of the world, to come into existence. Futuyma's claims are sufficiently unguarded that the unwary reader might be led to make a theological inference from what may simply be a biological statement.

2. Perhaps most importantly, if the world and its creatures developed purely by material, physical forces, it could not have been designed and has no purpose or goal. The fundamentalist, in contrast, believes that everything in the world, every species and every characteristic of every species, was designed by an intelligent, purposeful artificer, and that it was made for a purpose. Nowhere does this contrast apply with more force than to the human species. Some shrink from the conclusion that the human species was not

designed, has no purpose, and is the product of mere material mechanisms—but this seems to be the message of evolution.[25]

Here it is not clear whether Futuyma is simply alluding to incorrect inferences that might be drawn from evolution or if he in fact makes these incorrect inferences himself. Christians agree that in some meaningful sense God did design and make human beings for a purpose. Even though we may readily grant that material mechanisms may have been involved in forming the human species, human beings, on the Christian view, are not *solely* the product of these mechanisms. If Futuyma is claiming that human beings are not on earth for a purpose and were not designed by God but came into being *only* through physical-biological mechanisms, then he has drawn improper conclusions from a scientific theory. If Futuyma does not mean that, then he has once more expressed himself in such a way that the unwary reader could get the impression that biological evolution does, after all, imply that human beings are without purpose. This erroneous conclusion is one that Christians vigorously opposed to evolution have long been making. Futuyma does nothing at this point to correct that error or to reassure the reader otherwise.

3. Evolution wouldn't be such a controversial subject if it didn't touch on our perceptions of ourselves. In the Western tradition, humans are set apart from the natural world. The gap in mental and emotional powers between humans and animals is thought to be a profound, unbridgeable difference in kind. According to this anthropocentric, even egocentric tradition, the earth and its inhabitants were created to serve us. We are the special object of God's creative beneficence, so much so that he will even bend the natural world to our desires, and alter natural laws in response to our special pleading. Nothing could be more antithetical to such a world view than a science that tells us the earth is not the center of the universe; that life came and went for billions of years before man appeared on the scene; that living things and the human species itself originated by natural, impersonal causes rather than

the direct intervention of a Creator; that we are as much a part of nature as each of the millions of other species with which we share a common bond of inheritance.[26]

In this passage Futuyma pits scientific methodology and theory against a religious world view. Christians confess that humanity *is* the special object of God's creative beneficence. We do claim that God has given the created world to us for our good. We confess that God has given the heavenly bodies to us for signs and seasons and that he has given us other life forms for food. Such a confession in no way implies that the heavenly bodies and other life forms exist *only* for us.[27] We are puzzled as to how the scientific perspective can be antithetical to a world view in which human beings are the special objects of God's creative beneficence and the other organisms exist, at least in part, to serve us, if, as Futuyma has explained so well elsewhere, the scientific perspective is limited to addressing questions about the physical mechanisms of material patterns of behavior. Science, operating within its appropriately restricted domain, cannot decide whether or not human beings are special to God.

4. In the world of nature, there is neither good nor evil. The extinction of a comet astronomers recently sighted plunging into the sun is not a cosmic tragedy, it is just an event produced by mindless physical forces. Neither is the extinction of the pterodactyl tragic, nor is the struggle for existence that causes evolution either good or bad. It just is. Species arise throughout the ages, "but time and chance happeneth to them all."[28]

Perhaps Futuyma merely means here that from the scientific perspective, which by its very nature cannot make ethical judgments but only describes the world, natural events are neither good nor evil but just are. If that is all he intends to say, then we agree. But he appears to be saying more. To say that in the world of nature there is neither good nor evil is to make a metaphysical assertion. Such a claim should certainly not be made as a conclusion based on the findings of natural science. Moreover, there is a vast difference between the distinctly metaphysical statement that forces are "mindless" and a scientific statement which makes no claims about the mindless or personal nature of forces.

Many individual scientists are convinced that the "forces of nature" are personal in the sense that they are governed by a divine mind. Other scientists believe that there is nothing but matter and energy. For them forces are mindless and impersonal. But these philosophical biases of individual scientists are not the product of communal science. How could natural science ever test the notion of the mindlessness of force? How could science ever test the notion that a divine mind is directing the action of forces over a long term?

Thus even as careful a writer as Futuyma occasionally lapses into the error of transferring the methodological naturalism of natural science into an ontological naturalism which makes unwarranted metaphysical assertions about the ultimate character of reality.

In spite of the best intentions of writers to recognize the limits of natural science, the temptation to make metaphysical assertions as if they were the logical deductions from scientific discoveries is a strong temptation that is not easily avoided. Because they are not always aware that they are doing so, such writers rarely identify these metaphysical assertions as philosophical rather than scientific in nature. Rarely do they indicate, when they yield to temptation, that they are now about to express a personal religious conviction or conclusion that cannot be demonstrated on the basis of any scientific reasoning. Consequently, the reader of popular scientific writing must always be on guard whenever a writer begins to discuss the ultimate nature of reality, the nature of God, God's relationship to the world and man, or ethical standards. One can be sure that as soon as such happens we have left the realm of scientific theorizing and have entered the domain of philosophy or religion.

A MASQUERADE

OF

SCIENCE

8

T HE DUST JACKET TO P. W. ATKINS'S THE CREATION hails it as "an enthralling and poetic vision of modern science." Readers are further promised that they will "discover both the ultimate nature of the universe and the manner in which it came into being." In the preface the author himself tells us that "this is an account of the nature and the origin of the universe, but it is not just another book about astronomy or elementary particles."[1] Atkins wishes to deal only with the "central aspects of the universe . . . that are now open to scientific elucidation."[2] Consequently, to avoid the bewildering burden of detail, he chooses to "select from modern science the broad features of its explanations and implications."[3]

From these and similar comments, and from the numerous refer-

ences to physical phenomena and our contemporary scientific understanding of them, readers are encouraged to think of this as a book
whose subject matter lies squarely within the domain of modern natural *science*. While both the author and the publisher candidly admit
that this is a provocative and unusual book, its contents are still presented as a product of the contemporary scientific enterprise. Its conclusions claim *scientific* warrant; even its conjectures are offered as
implications of *science*. In fact, the principal goal of the book is to
demonstrate that the origin of the physical universe from nothing,
without the intervention of any external, nonphysical agent, lies within the grasp of scientific explanation. *The Creation* is a book which
claims to draw only from the well of natural science and the reservoir
of its logical implications.

That claim, however, must be rejected. This is not an authentic
product of natural science. Science is its mask, not its face. The domain of the book's principal thesis lies far beyond the borders of
natural science. The thesis of this volume is worthy of critical examination, but only after its arena of discourse has been properly identified. For the moment, I wish only to demonstrate that the central
thesis of *The Creation* does *not* reside within the domain of the natural
sciences.

To facilitate this demonstration, let us establish some working def-
initions of important terms so that certain crucial distinctions can be
made. Following the example of cosmologist Edward R. Harrison,[4] I
find it fruitful to distinguish between *Universe* and *universe*. By *Universe*
I shall mean the unified and coherent whole of reality—all that exists,
encompassing such categories as deity, material things, persons and
ideas, and including a system of relationships which specify the status
of each member relative to other members. The Universe in its full-
ness, however, is beyond human comprehension; therefore, we must
be content to construct models, mental pictures of the Universe of
which we are a part. We shall use the word *universe* to represent a
humanly constructed model of the Universe.

The concept of universe varies from culture to culture and from age to age. For most of us, our concept of universe—our world view—is more an inheritance, historically and culturally conditioned, than a product of individual reflection. As members of a culture whose inheritance is drawn from many differing world-view traditions, one of our tasks is to become aware of the diverse concepts of universe present in our culture, to distinguish them from one another and to distinguish each of them from the Universe we seek to know.

In contemporary usage, however, the term *universe* is commonly employed to refer only to the physical universe. The physical universe is that component of one's universe (one's model of reality) that is accessible to the natural sciences. The universe constructed by the natural sciences is a structured and dynamically interacting system of matter, radiation, energy, space-time and like constituents. To call attention to the importance of recognizing the restricted definition of the physical universe, Harrison introduces the "containment principle," which states: "The physical universe contains everything that is physical and nothing else."[5] Though this may appear so obvious as not to require an explicit statement, it is frequently overlooked.

Natural science, as it has come to be defined by the professional scientific community, and as manifested by the character of professional scientific literature, is limited to the study of the physical universe. The domain of contemporary natural science, we said in chapter one, is the inherent intelligibility of the physical universe. As Harrison puts it, "Modern [scientific] cosmology studies a physical universe that includes all that is physical and excludes all that is nonphysical."[6]

Note carefully: this is not to say that nonphysical entities do not exist or that they are not significant. Harrison's description of scientific cosmology is simply calling attention to the limited domain of the natural sciences. The sciences neither affirm nor deny the existence of a nonphysical realm; they choose, rather, to remain silent. The nonphysical realm has been consciously excluded from the domain of scientific investigation. If one wishes to affirm belief in a deity who is the Creator of the physical universe, one may not claim *scientific* warrant for that belief. Similarly, if one wishes to deny the existence of anything outside of the physical universe, one must recognize that such a metaphysical assertion cannot be warranted by *scientific* investigation.

The study of the inherent intelligibility of the physical universe is incapable of determining whether that universe is self-existent or is dependent on a divine Creator for its existence. The basis for such a metaphysical choice lies outside of the domain of natural science. To be cognizant of the limited domain of science is a matter of competence; to honor the boundary of that domain is a matter of integrity.

If the domain of natural science is the inherent intelligibility of the physical universe, can Atkins's book, *The Creation,* be considered a product of the scientific enterprise? Clearly not. The chief topic of *The Creation* is the ultimate question of cosmogenesis: What is the source, or cause, of the existence of the physical universe? *

As Atkins states in the preface, "My aim is to argue that the universe can come into existence without intervention, and that there is no *need* to invoke the idea of a Supreme Being in one of its numerous manifestations."[7] And what does Atkins offer the reader as the basis for his argumentation? None other than the results of *natural science.* "What I am trying to do, it should always be remembered, is to show that deep questions about cosmogony [by which he means cosmogenesis] can be asked, that in some cases they have already been answered, and that in others *science* is pointing to the type of answer that may be forthcoming quite soon."[8] Elsewhere he wishes the reader to "admit that *science* is extraordinarily strong and . . . that it appears

---

*Note: Atkins uses the word *cosmogony* rather than *cosmogenesis.* I prefer, however, to employ Harrison's distinction between *cosmogony* (the study of the formation of material systems within the physical universe, such as galaxies, stars and planets) and *cosmogenesis* (the study dealing with the origin—in the sense of source or cause—of the existence of the physical universe as a whole).[9]

to be on the edge of explaining everything."[10]

To assert that science has the potential for explaining everything, including cosmogenesis, constitutes a grievous misrepresentation of the scientific enterprise. Perhaps Atkins is merely semantically trapped by his own dogmatic reductionism. For Atkins, the physical universe is all there is. Therefore, if science is the study of the physical universe, then science is the study of all there is.

But I believe the shortcomings of Atkins's claims are more serious than this semantic ambiguity. By denying the existence of anything outside of the realm of physical phenomena, he equates the Universe with the physical universe modeled by contemporary science. Furthermore, he wishes to warrant that denial by appeal to the results of scientific investigation. However, as we have already noted, natural science is inherently incapable of warranting either the denial or the affirmation of a nonphysical realm. Thus, Atkins must own either of two major shortcomings in his argumentation: (1) he is employing, without candidly informing his readers, an unconventional definition of natural science; or (2) he is illegitimately claiming scientific warrant for his metaphysical assertions concerning the contents of the Universe.

Atkins's *The Creation* may be "an enthralling and poetic vision," but it surely is *not* the product of modern natural science. Neither can its conclusions be hailed as "implications" of contemporary science. Atkins's assertions will have to be judged on their own merits. Any appeal to the power or prestige of natural science is entirely unwarranted and must be rejected as grossly misleading. Atkins is no doubt welcome to express his personal world view, but his readers certainly deserve to be more accurately and honestly informed concerning the source of that perspective. Natural science is not the source of Atkins's beliefs. For him to admit this openly would constitute an admirable display of both personal and professional integrity. For him to deny it is to cover the face of his naturalistic creed with the mask of natural science.

The Face Unmasked: Naturalism

The Creation does not offer its readers a system of scientific theories for evaluation by the conventional criteria of professional natural science. Rather, it presents readers with P. W. Atkins's attempt to find scientific warrant for his personal world view—his naturalistic creed. While Atkins does employ arguments which refer to scientific theories, his purpose is not to evaluate the theories per se, but to convince readers that (to use Harrison's terminology) the Universe contains no more than the physical universe.

The principal objective of *The Creation* is to persuade its readers that there is no divine Creator; that the physical universe has created itself from absolutely nothing; that the universe is autonomous (self-regulated, not divinely governed); that neither the universe nor we who inhabit it have any ultimate value or significance; and that the existence and history of the corporeal cosmos is utterly without purpose. Atkins's message is that we are *nothing more* than complex assemblages of self-created matter, that we are merely "the children of aimless chance."[11]

Behind the mask of natural science we find the face of naturalism. Although natural science self-consciously restricts its domain to the inherent intelligibility of the physical universe, naturalism makes bold creedal assertions concerning the status of the physical universe relative to deity and the implications of that status for questions concerning the origin, governance, value and purpose of the universe.

Atkins's brand of naturalism might also be called "reductive materialism," the belief that all of reality can be reduced to the material (physical) world and that all real phenomena can be understood in terms of material behavior alone. According to Atkins, there is no realm of deity, no God, no Creator. Furthermore, what we are tempted to perceive as a meaningful realm of human self-consciousness or human thought is fully reducible to the complex electrochemical processes that take place in those marvelous molecular machines that we call the human brain. Atkins's concept of reality resonates with that of Carl Sagan who equates the Cosmos with the physical universe, and for whom "The Cosmos is all that is or ever was or ever will be."[12]

The only kind of deity considered by Atkins in *The Creation* is a deistic version of a creator whose sole function is to effect, by "intervention," the inception of the physical world. But even this distant echo of deity is silenced by Atkins. His strategy is to present a series of increasingly strong assertions that the task of such a creator is far smaller than traditionally believed; in fact, according to Atkins, it is now scientifically demonstrable (or very nearly so) that such a creator has essentially nothing to do and can therefore be an "infinitely lazy creator."

For Atkins, "the only way of explaining the creation is to show that the creator had absolutely no job at all to do, and so might as well not have existed."[13] Atkins leads the reader on a "journey to discover . . . the manner in which [the universe] came into being."[14] Toward the end of this journey the reader is informed that "we have been back to the time before time, and have tracked the infinitely lazy creator to his lair (he is, of course, not there)."[15] Atkins thereby presumes to have fulfilled his earlier promise to show "how a non-existent creator can be allowed to evaporate into nothing and to disappear from the scene."[16]

While I fully reject Atkins's atheistic world view, nevertheless I think he has performed a valuable service by demonstrating where a consistently naturalistic perspective leads—to a concept of a completely meaningless existence. Having rejected the existence of God, even of an infinitely lazy deistic type of creator, Atkins must search for meaning and significance for humanity in purely materialistic terms. Quite appropriately, Atkins finds nothing significant in a Universe without God or in a humanity unrelated to deity. The implications of this insignificance for the life of a person or of a community would be of utmost importance, but Atkins chooses not to explore this territory.

Humanity, as presented in *The Creation,* has no ultimate significance. The human being is no more than a complex arrangement of elemental atoms. Listen to Atkins profess his own insignificance:

> If there are atoms there will in due course be molecules; and if there are molecules on warm, wet platforms, there will in due course be elephants. (p. 5)
>
> . . . elephants, and things resembling elephants will in due course be found roaming through the countryside. (p. 3)
>
> Some of the things resembling elephants will be men. They are equally unimportant. . . . Their special but not significant function is that they are able to act as commentators on the nature, content, structure, and source of the universe and that, as a sideline, they can devise and take pleasure from communicable fantasies. (p. 3)
>
> Man and his counterparts elsewhere are merely elephants with a tendency to hubris. We are fragments of the universe, elephants happily free to roam intellectually as well as spatially. As elaborate outcrops of the physical world, *and no more than that* we are no more necessary to its existence than is a breeze. (p. 85, emphasis added)

Presumably, if either the readers or the writer of these words has a sense of significance, a sense of being more than a mere material machine, even that is a delusion arising out of electronic noise in the brain's electrochemical machinery.

The heart of a world view—a creed—is a set of concepts concerning the relative status of God, humanity and the physical world. Atkins's naturalism (or reductive materialism) asserts a Universe without deity, a Universe composed wholly of things physical. Its concept of the human person is thoroughly mechanistic. Humanity is an intriguing but insignificant assemblage of atoms arranged into a structure of sufficient complexity to experience the illusion of significance. The only reality is the physical world, but, as we shall see later, even that physical world, according to Atkins, is but a variant form of "nothing." The physical world has the status of "all there is." As the ultimate reality, the physical universe stands in place of God, making his existence an unnecessary conjecture, in Atkins's judgment.

If, by virtue of its being all that exists, the physical universe has the status of ultimate reality, then it cannot owe its existence to any other being. The universe of naturalism must be self-originating. For this reason, I surmise, Atkins devotes the bulk of his effort in *The Creation* to the development of an argument for the credibility of a self-originating universe—one that is able to create itself from nothing (whatever that may mean). Having speculated (or we might say, "devised a communicable fantasy") concerning the existence of a primordial "dust" of spacelike and timelike points not yet organized into four-dimensional space-time as we know it, Atkins says: "But we need one more concept, a concept able to account for the emergence of things out of nothing."[17] Atkins expresses a deep faith that natural science is capable of providing such a concept, and he thinks "we can see the rudiments of the self-inception of the world."[18]

What are the ingredients of this self-inception concept?

There are two ingredients. First we need the points that are to assemble into patterns defining space and time.

Then we need the points that separate from their opposites by virtue of the pattern of time. Time lends life to the points; the points lend life to time. Time brought the points into being, and the points brought time into being. This is the cosmic bootstrap. (p. 111)

In a word, the central speculation is that space-time generates its own dust in the process of its own self-assembly. The universe can emerge out of nothing without intervention. By chance. (p. 113)

Atkins is displaying honesty by identifying this as *speculation*. Further clarification, however, is essential. In the context of the discussion, readers may be misled into thinking of this self-inception concept as being a *scientific* speculation. Such, however, is not the case at all. As a conjecture concerning the ultimate source and nature of reality, this is a *metaphysical* speculation, with religious implications. Atkins's "enthralling and poetic vision" must be perceived as a profession of his naturalistic creed, not as a specimen of scientific theorizing. Atkins's vision is indeed an intriguing speculation. But it must be seen as a religious conjecture concerning the implication of his reductive materialism for the source of existence itself. Such a matter is not a concern of professional natural science, but a tenet of Atkins's naturalistic creed.

Within the framework of a theistic world view, the physical universe is perceived as being totally dependent on the sovereign Creator for both its existence and its governance. The Bible, for example, speaks of God the Creator not only as the originator of the created world, but also as its governor. Even the behavior of inanimate material systems is ultimately governed by divine action.

This is not to say that the Creator dictates every physical event, thereby destroying the possibility of human responsibility. Rather, in a manner consistent with biblical talk concerning God's active presence in his created world, we seek to recognize that the source of governance and the source of existence for the physical world are identical—the activity of its divine Creator. The character of divine governance, as depicted in the Bible, precludes the meaninglessness inherent in either total chaos or absolute dictation. Furthermore, the reality of divine governance ensures that cosmic history will achieve the ultimate purposes of the Creator for his creation.

According to the perspective of reductive materialism, however, the physical universe must be autonomous. If the self-originated material world is all there is, then its behavior must be self-governed. The natural sciences excel in discovering the patterns of material behavior; we often refer to these patterns as the "laws of nature." Atkins, however, appears to be uncomfortable with talk about "laws" or "rules" (perhaps this is because a reference to rules so readily suggests the existence of a rule-giver) and argues that a thing's *behavior* is fully determined by its *nature*. If it is a thing's nature to act in a certain way, its action need not be regulated by a creator-imposed rule. Says Atkins: "An infinitely lazy creator would avoid the specification of rules if an entity's nature alone could govern its behavior."[19]

Following this introduction to the topic of governance, Atkins proceeds to argue his case that even rules of material behavior are an illusion. The patterns of behavior exhibited by light or particles, claims Atkins, are not to be seen as evidence for their response to a governing power, but rather as a product of their complete freedom to explore all possible paths of activity. The resulting patterns of behavior are merely an artifact of survival. Other possible paths of behavior are inherently self-annihilating. The kind of behavior that survives forms a pattern, thereby giving the illusion of obeying a rule.

Although Atkins has devised a fascinating scenario for the generation of patterns in material behavior, he has not been able to avoid the question of governance. Whereas traditional discussions may have distinguished between a thing's *properties* and its *behavior,* Atkins has chosen to combine both of these qualities into a thing's *nature.* Whereas other adherents of naturalism might speak of autonomous material behavior, Atkins employs a concept of self-generated nature.

The basic question, however, remains: Does the source of a thing's nature (including the manner of its behavior) reside wholly within the physical universe, or does a thing's nature originate in the action of an agent distinctly different from the physical universe—a divine Creator, for example? As in the case for origin of existence, so also the question of governance (origin of behavior) is a profoundly metaphysical and religious question. Atkins's answer is not the product of scientific theorizing; it is a tenet of his naturalistic creed. Atkins is entitled to profess his creed, but in order to evaluate it appropriately we must be careful to distinguish creedal assertions from scientific conclusions. The evaluation of scientific theories is an activity appropriate for the science classroom. The evaluation of religious perspectives, however, might better be carried out in a different context.

Closely related to the question of governance is the question of purpose. Is there a purpose for the existence of the universe and the course of cosmic history? Consistent with his reductive materialism, Atkins considers purpose to be an illusion. Basing his perspective on his interpretation of the second law of thermodynamics, Atkins asserts that, "All change . . . arises from an underlying collapse into chaos. We shall see that what may appear to us to be motive and purpose is in fact ultimately motiveless, purposeless decay."[20] According to Atkins, *nothing* is exempt from this indictment. "Everything is driven by motiveless, purposeless decay."[21]

How then does it happen that the illusion of motive, or purpose or mind appears so prevalent in the world? Speaking about the atomic and molecular activity that takes place in the brain, Atkins says: "That this motiveless, purposeless, mindless activity emerges into the world as motive and purpose, and constitutes a mind, is wholly due to the complexity of its organization."[22]

If Atkins were to say that natural science is incapable of dealing with questions of ultimate purpose, that would be an appropriate recognition of the limited domain of the natural sciences. Science, performed with integrity, is eager to recognize its own limitations in both domain and methodology. Atkins, however, makes assertions far outside of those limits. Having failed to find a way to comprehend motive, purpose or mind in wholly physical terms, Atkins asserts that such concepts are no more than illusions of complexity. In essence, Atkins would have readers believe that if something cannot be comprehended within the categories accessible to the natural sciences, then it simply does not exist. By now it should be clear that such a belief cannot be warranted by appeal to the natural sciences; it is no more than an assertion of reductive materialism.

The principal thesis of *The Creation* is that the physical universe is the self-originating, self-sustaining, self-governing, motiveless, purposeless, mindless sum total of all reality. Consequently, *The Creation* must be seen as Atkins's profession of faith, his statement of belief in reductive materialism, his naturalistic creed. But insofar as Atkins attempts to employ the results of natural science to provide warrant (or at least the appearance of warrant) for his creedal commitments, *The Creation* functions as an exemplar of naturalistic folk science.

Creationist folk science (more commonly called "creation-science") strives to warrant its belief in a particular concept of divine creation by means of unconventional interpretations of selected empirical data. Naturalistic folk science seeks to warrant its belief in reductive materialism by constructing arguments which have the appearance of being logical extrapolations from the results of professional natural science. In neither case are the boundaries of the domain of natural science honored. In both cases science has become indentured in the service of an ideological or religious commitment. Behind the mask of numerous references to scientific investigation we find the face of Atkins's naturalistic creed.

SAGAN'S COSMOS: SCIENCE EDUCATION OR RELIGIOUS THEATER?

9

BILLIONS AND BILLIONS OF STARS IN EACH OF BILlions and billions of galaxies. In 1980 Cornell astronomer Carl Sagan gave to the number *billion* (initiated with an exploding *b*) a heightened level of familiarity among the viewers of his public television series, "Cosmos."

Captivated by breath-taking cosmic vistas, soul-stirring background music and mind-boggling data from the natural sciences, an estimated ten million viewers joined Sagan on his "personal voyage" through the Cosmos. (Drawing in part on the ancient Greek concept of a harmoniously regulated, and therefore intelligible, world, Sagan persistently employed the term *Cosmos* as the proper name for the physical universe that is the object of scientific scrutiny and the focus of Sagan's concern.) Viewers were informed of the varied contents and

vast dimensions of the universe; and they were shown the contemporary picture of cosmic history—a history beginning with the Big Bang
and progressively unfolding with the appearance of galaxies, stars,
planets, living things and, finally, a species characterized by Sagan as
self-conscious molecular machines capable of pondering the vast Cosmos from which they arose. This is the species of persons who now
ask, Where are we? and, far more profoundly, Who are we?

"Cosmos" was well grounded in the results of scientific investigation. Sagan has excellent credentials as a knowledgeable practicing
scientist, and he draws deeply from the well of contemporary scientific
theory and from the pool of observational data. Viewers could rest
assured that the science component of "Cosmos" was representative
of what the professional scientific community has come to know about
the physical universe in which we live. Furthermore, with a multimil-
lion-dollar budget and a large and skilled production staff, Sagan was
able to present the products of scientific investigation in a strikingly
vivid and colorful manner. "Cosmos" was able to attract and hold the
attention of viewers with a tenacity nearly unrivalled in the public
television sector.

There were, of course, some shortcomings. The pace of the presentation varied considerably. At times the flow of technical information
was like a rushing stream. Some viewers must have felt as if they were
being asked to take a drink from a fire hose. At other times, particularly in some of the historical dramatizations, the stream ran nearly
dry.

"Cosmos" also suffered from a very common malady of popularized
science: overstating the degree of certainty in many parts of the contemporary scientific picture. In the first episode, Sagan made a significant promise to his viewers. "We will be careful," he said, "to distinguish speculation from fact." And on some occasions such distinctions
were made. In the context of a discussion of chemical evolution,
Sagan said: "There is still much to be understood about the origin of
life, including the origin of the genetic code."[1] But on numerous other

occasions Sagan neglected to remind his viewers of the tentative character of much of today's understanding of cosmic structure, behavior and formative history.

Persons who are thoroughly familiar with the nature of the scientific enterprise need not be repeatedly reminded of the tentativeness that characterizes scientific theorizing, especially on the matter of historical reconstruction, but others—the vast majority, I suggest— need guidance. Educating the nonspecialist on this matter may be difficult, but the general public needs to gain some appreciation for the process of scientific theory evaluation. Judging the merits of a scientific theory must be viewed as the employment of both good common sense and healthy skepticism in an effort to avoid both the propagation of inflexible dogma and the careless expression of groundless opinion.

"Cosmos" as Religious Theater

Having called attention to certain educational needs we should now inquire, Was science education the principal goal of "Cosmos"? In my judgment, it was not. Although the results of contemporary science played a prominent role throughout the entire series, I believe that "Cosmos" functioned most powerfully as *religious theater,* that is, as a dramatic presentation of information, concepts and ideas organized around a strongly religious agenda. Furthermore, while recognizing that Sagan deserves considerable credit for providing his audience with a vividly illustrated presentation of the contemporary, scientifically derived picture of the physical universe, I believe that it was the provocative religious agenda and its theatrical format that most captivated the viewing audience.

Such bold statements call for substantiation, so let us briefly consider the religion, the theater and the agenda of Sagan's "Cosmos."

The religion: The religious faith that permeated the "Cosmos" series is modern Western naturalism—the perspective formed by the wedding of materialistic monism (there is only one form of reality: matter) and exclusivist scientism (there is only one way to learn about reality: natural science). Sagan quoted Democritus of Abdera as saying, "Nothing exists but atoms and the void."[2] Standing solidly in the materialist tradition of Democritus, Sagan of Brooklyn opened "Cosmos" with the fundamental tenet of naturalistic religion, "The Cosmos is all that is or ever was or ever will be."[3] The physical universe was asserted to be the only reality; it was assumed that there exists no being or realm that transcends the material world.

As the only reality, the Cosmos must serve to inspire whatever religious stirrings we humans experience. Thus, immediately following the opening statement of the materialist creed, Sagan declared: "Our feeblest contemplations of the Cosmos stir us—there is a tingling in the spine, a catch in the voice, a faint sensation, as if a distant memory, of falling from a height. We know we are approaching the greatest of mysteries."[4]

But what of humanity and human thought? Are these nothing more than instances of complex atomic behavior? Expressing considerable admiration of the insights of Democritus, Sagan wrote, "He taught that perception—the reason, say, I think there is a pen in my hand—was a purely physical and mechanistic process; that thinking and feeling were attributes of matter put together in a sufficiently fine and complex way and not due to some spirit infused into matter by the gods."[5] The perspective on the ultimate character and identity of human beings offered in "Cosmos" is clearly a modernized version of the view of Democritus: we are marvelous molecular machines—somehow deserving of awe, but yet only machines. Said Sagan,

> I am a collection of water, calcium and organic molecules called Carl Sagan. You are a collection of almost identical molecules with a different collective label. But is that all? Is there nothing in here but molecules? Some people find this idea somehow demeaning to human dignity. For myself, I find it elevating that our universe permits the evolution of molecular machines as intricate and subtle as we.[6]

Now, if only the physical universe is real, what about the concept of God, or of gods? A candid statement of the materialist faith would be that neither God nor gods exist, period. Discreetly avoiding such a direct expression of atheism, Sagan chose to put this perspective in the form of suggestive questions and of hypothetical statements. For example, after describing the Hindu concept of the universe being the realized form of a divine dream, Sagan suggested, "These great ideas are tempered by another, perhaps still greater. It is said that men may not be the dreams of the gods, but rather that the gods are the dreams of men."[7] Deity, Sagan suggests, is nothing more than a human invention; and human invention, recall, is nothing more than the peculiar output of a complex molecular machine. God is thus reduced to a figment of mechanistic molecular imagination.

Seen as requiring nothing beyond itself as the cause of its existence, or as the governor of its behavior, or as the source of its value and purpose, the Cosmos of the materialist faith must perform many of the functions customarily thought to be dependent on divine action. In that sense the physical universe becomes a material substitute for traditional deities.

Furthermore, the reverence people once directed toward deity, they should now, in the materialist religion, direct toward the Cosmos itself. While in the Judeo-Christian tradition human beings are seen as having their ultimate identity as children of God, "Cosmos" identified the human race entirely in material terms. "We are," said Sagan, "in the most profound sense, children of the Cosmos."[8] And in the video script Sagan professed, "Our ancestors worshiped the Sun, and they were far from foolish. It makes good sense to revere the Sun and the stars because we are their children." Sagan's language may be metaphorical, but the metaphor expresses a creedal tenet. God and Cosmos are no longer distinct; one has been absorbed into the other.

Now, if the physical world were all there is, then it would be easy to conclude that science is the principal, perhaps even exclusive, means of attaining any knowledge of reality. As we have said already, the natural sciences, when operating within their legitimate domain, provide a powerful means of seeking answers to questions drawn from appropriate categories. Although the sciences cannot deal with *all* questions, they function well in our search for answers to *appropriate* questions (questions regarding the inherent intelligibility of the physical universe). The perspective of science offered in "Cosmos" rightfully called attention to the power of scientific investigation but conspicuously omitted reference to any limitation of domain, asserting instead *unrestricted applicability*. Listen to this litany of praise for the unbounded reach of the scientific approach in the search for understanding our origins:

> Its only sacred truth is that there are no sacred truths. All assumptions must be critically examined; arguments from authority are worthless. Whatever is inconsistent with the facts, however fond of it we are, must be discarded or revised. Science is not perfect. It's often misused. It's only a tool. But it's the best tool we have, self-correcting, ever-changing, *applicable to everything*. With this tool we vanquish the impossible.[9]

Elsewhere, in another discussion which failed to distinguish between the question of *origin* and questions about *formative history*, Sagan said:

> Every human generation has asked about the origin and fate of the Cosmos. Ours is the first generation [because of its scientific prowess] with a real chance of finding some of the answers. One way or another, we are poised on the edge of forever.[10]

Clearly, then, the "Cosmos" series displayed throughout, from the opening line forward, a specific and powerful religious perspective that functioned as the framework for the interpretation of scientific and historical data. It was the nontheistic religion of modern Western naturalism: the physical world is the ultimate reality, and natural science is the only avenue to understanding. Reality was reduced to matter alone, and a fittingly bounded respect for science was replaced by an unrestrained scientism.

The theater: The religious dimension of "Cosmos" was evident not only in its conceptual content but also in its theatrical format. "Cosmos" was powerful theater that effectively maintained an aura of religious awe. The music, for example, functioned with remarkable success to maintain a mood that was haunting, mystical, ethereal, almost worshipful. And Sagan's "ship of the imagination" that carried him on his personal voyage through the Cosmos had the unmistakable appearance of a cathedral, complete with a futuristic variant of Gothic architecture and with a pulpitlike control station well suited for priestly pronouncements.

The format of "Cosmos" bore little resemblance to what would be found in a science classroom. The content of "Cosmos" had considerable educational value, but in genre this television production must be classified as theater—theater with a strongly religious agenda, a subtle but nonetheless effective form of "televangelism."

The agenda: Among the many goals which could be identified as comprising the religious agenda of "Cosmos," we will focus here on three that are judged to be especially important.

1. To imply that a naturalistic religious perspective is warranted by natural science.

More by persistent implication than by candid statement, "Cosmos" very effectively promoted the idea that a naturalistic *world view* (a perspective on all of reality) is but a simple, logical extension of the scientific *world picture* (a description of the physical universe only). Typical of this approach is the argument that if the physical universe displays an intelligible unity and coherence, then the "god-hypothesis" is unnecessary; and if unnecessary, then to be discarded—surgically removed by Ockham's razor of philosophical economy.* In a

---

Ockham's razor, a principle in science and philosophy, states that the number of assumptions employed to explain something should not be multiplied needlessly. This means that the simplest of two or more competing theories is preferable and that an explanation of unknown phenomena should first be attempted in terms of what is already known.

discussion concerning the early Greek discovery of patterned behavior that is accessible to empirical investigation, Sagan performed some of this surgery.

The Babylonian Marduk and the Greek Zeus was each considered master of the sky and king of the gods. You might decide that Marduk and Zeus were really the same. You might also decide, since they had quite different attributes, that one of them was merely invented by the priests. But if one, why not both?

And so it was that the great idea arose, the realization that there might be a way to know the world without the god hypothesis; that there might be principles, forces, laws of nature through which the world could be understood without attributing the fall of every sparrow to a direct intervention of Zeus.[11]

Note carefully the essential element in this argument: If there are intelligible regularities of physical *behavior* that can be discovered by empirical science, then the idea of divine *governance* must be eliminated. Instead of entertaining the idea that divine governance is orderly and noncapricious in character, Sagan chose to eliminate the concept of divine governance entirely. Clearly, that was a religious choice, not a scientific conclusion.

The essential distinction between *behavior* and *governance* appears not to have functioned in this discussion. By failing to give recognition to this distinction, the rhetoric of "Cosmos" strongly implied that the scientific discovery of regular patterns of physical behavior provides sufficient warrant—the crucial proof, if you prefer—for a naturalistic world view. From this it was a relatively short step to the next major item on the religious agenda of "Cosmos":

2. *To assert that this naturalistic religion has triumphed over all forms of theistic religion.*

On numerous occasions "Cosmos" declared the naturalistic perspective to be superior to any form of theism. Naturalism, presumably based solely on the results of empirical science, was alleged to provide superior answers to the same questions as those addressed by theism, presumably based only on human imagination, superstition and fear. Were this the case, then, naturalism would provide us with keener insights concerning our identity—who we are. Listen to some of the triumphalist rhetoric to be found in "Cosmos":

> We are, almost all of us, descended from people who responded to the dangers of existence by inventing stories about unpredictable or disgruntled deities. For a long time the human instinct to understand was thwarted by facile religious explanations.[12]

> For thousands of years humans were oppressed—as some of us still are—by the notion that the universe is a marionette whose strings are pulled by a god or gods, unseen and inscrutable.[13]

In a discussion of the rise of systematic science in ancient Greece, Sagan hailed Thales for his attempt to understand the world in wholly naturalistic terms. After describing Thales's theory about the central role played by water, Sagan commented:

> Whether Thales's conclusion was correct is not as important as his approach: the material world was not made by the gods, but instead was the work of material forces interacting in Nature.[14]

In a later episode on cosmology "Cosmos" offered still more comparisons of theistic and naturalistic perspectives. One striking and important feature of these comparisons was Sagan's working assumption that scientific cosmology and theological cosmology are concerned with the same questions. This fallacious equating of agendas was necessary, of course, if the scientific picture was to be offered as a superior successor to any theological perspective. As was the case for the behavior/governance distinction, "Cosmos" also failed utterly to recognize the essential distinction between *origin* and *formation*. Following a series of quotations from the creation mythology of various ancient cultures, Sagan asserted that these examples of theological cosmology and the Big Bang model of modern scientific cosmology, though they are quite different in quality, belong in the same category.

> These myths are tributes to human audacity. The chief difference

between them and our modern scientific myth of the Big Bang is that science is self-questioning, and that we can perform experiments and observations to test our ideas.[15]

In the video version Sagan said, "The Big Bang is our modern scientific creation myth. It comes from the same human need to solve the cosmological riddle." The fact that theological cosmology and scientific cosmology have remarkably different agendas was completely overlooked in these manifestations of the triumphalist agenda of "Cosmos." In one of his most direct attacks on the theological concept of creation, Sagan once again employed the weapon of Ockham's razor. The Creator's existence was dismissed as an awkward and unnecessary hypothesis that must be cut out in a move toward philosophical frugality.

> If the general picture of an expanding universe and a Big Bang is correct, we must then confront still more difficult questions. What were conditions like at the time of the Big Bang? Was there a tiny universe, devoid of all matter and then the matter suddenly created from nothing? How does *that* happen? In many cultures it is customary to answer that God created the universe out of nothing. But this is mere temporizing. If we wish courageously to pursue the question, we must, of course ask next where God comes from. And if we decide this to be unanswerable, why not save a step and decide that the origin of the universe is an unanswerable question? Or, if we say that God has always existed, why not save a step and conclude that the universe has always existed?[16]

Once again the viewer was urged to see naturalism as the triumphant victor over theism. This was by no means a simple lesson in science education. This was powerful religious theater.

But what was the point of this drama? In what way might a naturalistic religion function? Proposing an answer to this question provided yet another major item on the religious agenda of "Cosmos":

3. To promote the hope that a naturalistic religious perspective will inspire in the human race a loyalty to the Cosmos and a commitment to care for the preservation of both self and environment.

In a number of places Sagan expressed an admirable concern for conserving natural resources and for maintaining a high-quality environment for human life. Recognizing the cost of putting that concern into action, Sagan said:

> Our generation must choose. Which do we value more? Short term profits or the long term habitability of our own planetary home? . . . If a visitor arrived from another world, what account would we give of our stewardship of the planet Earth?[17]

But Sagan's use of terms like *value* and *stewardship* raise some interesting questions. On what basis is *value* determined? To whom are we responsible as *stewards?* A naturalistic religious perspective requires that the answers to these questions be found entirely within the physical universe. Consistent with his dream of a scientifically informed Utopia based solely on a cosmic consciousness, Sagan asserted that, "Humans everywhere share the same goals when the context is large enough. And the study of the Cosmos provides the largest possible context."[18] Having excluded deity from the real world, Sagan must rely on the physical universe as the sole source of significance and as the sole object of one's loyalties. In the closing lines of the series Sagan offered this inward-directed perspective on our identity and our function:

> For we are the local embodiment of a Cosmos grown to self-awareness. We have begun to contemplate our origins: starstuff pondering the stars; organized assemblages of ten billion billion billion atoms considering the evolution of atoms; tracing the long journey by which, here at least consciousness arose. Our loyalties are to the species and the planet. *We* speak for Earth. Our obligation to survive is owed not just to ourselves but also to that Cosmos, ancient and vast, from which we spring.[19]

Thus *value* must be expressed in the currency of species preservation and one's *stewardship* must be an expression of loyal obligation to the Cosmos itself.

As a general rule, the attitude expressed in "Cosmos" was one of hopefulness that a wholly naturalistic religion and a loyalty to the universe alone will provide a sufficient basis for a satisfying sense of meaning and significance. But yet within this same work one finds the seeds of insignificance and disillusionment.

> That we live in a universe which permits life is remarkable. That we live in one which destroys galaxies and stars and worlds is also remarkable. The universe seems neither benign nor hostile, merely *indifferent* to the concerns of such *puny creatures* as we.[20]

In a number of instances Sagan called us to be loyal and reverent toward the Cosmos. But if that Cosmos is itself both impersonal and indifferent to our human concerns, what satisfaction can possibly be derived from such loyalty? Where the naturalistic religious agenda sought to plant hope we find sprouting the seeds of futility.

Science Misrepresented

Sagan deserves to be credited, we said, for his knowledgeable and vividly illustrated presentation of the contemporary scientific world picture. Throughout the "Cosmos" series, viewers were provided with very informative descriptions of the contents, structure, behavior and history of the physical universe.

But in spite of our recognition of these praiseworthy features, we would argue that the fundamental character of the scientific enterprise was egregiously misrepresented in "Cosmos." Our principal criticism is that "Cosmos" failed to honor the boundaries of science's limited domain of applicability. What Sagan presented in this work was not merely a *world picture,* but a *world view*—not merely a scientific description of the physical component of reality, but a naturalistic religious perspective on the whole of reality. Furthermore, the naturalistic world view presented in "Cosmos" was treated as if it were but a logical extension of natural science, thus misrepresenting science as if it were capable of providing a sufficient warrant for rejecting any theistic perspective on our existence and our experience.

Natural science transformed into naturalistic scientism. When the boundaries of the scientific domain are no longer honored, science is soon transformed into scient*ism*. Science is treated as if it were "applicable to everything," to use Sagan's words. The spirit that pervaded "Cosmos" is that our search for answers to questions regarding our identity, our significance, even the source of our existence, are entirely dependent on the natural sciences. The only source of knowledge recognized by "Cosmos" is the physical universe. The only avenue to understanding accepted by "Cosmos" is scientific investigation.

What Sagan failed to point out is that, although natural science chooses to limit the object of its investigation to the physical universe, that does not provide any warrant for asserting that "the Cosmos is all there is or ever was or ever will be."[21] Clearly, such a statement cannot be a conclusion of natural science. Rather, it is the statement of religious faith on which the naturalism of "Cosmos" is founded. Had that distinction between metaphysical assumption and scientific conclusion been candidly made, the religious agenda of "Cosmos" would have been more obvious from the outset.

Science presented as victor over religion. Throughout "Cosmos" the warfare metaphor was consistently used to characterize the relationship of science to theistic religion. Ignoring the distinction between *behavior* and *governance,* Sagan treated scientific descriptions of physical behavior as if they were direct competitors to religious concepts of divine governance. Ignoring the distinction between *formation* and *origin,* Sagan treated scientific descriptions of the formative history of the universe as if they were superior replacements for the theistic concept that God is the source for the very existence of the universe.

More could be said to substantiate and reinforce our criticisms of the way in which "Cosmos" caricatured the scientific enterprise, but by this time the point should be clear. By failing to honor the boundaries of the scientific domain, by transforming natural science into naturalistic scientism and by presenting science as the victor over theism, "Cosmos" misrepresented the character of the scientific enterprise. Although the stage was set for an enriching experience in science education, what actually occurred was religious theater—an evangelistic crusade for modern Western naturalism.

EPILOGUE
FOLK SCIENCE:
THE FACE BEHIND
THE MASK

WE ALL HAVE CONCERN FOR MATTERS BEYOND THE limited domain of natural science. Thus we often puzzle about how the results of science may be related to those extrascientific concerns. How, for example, are the results of scientific investigation to be employed as we assemble a comprehensive world view—a perspective in which certain creedal or religious commitments play a prominent role?

In an earlier chapter we strongly discouraged the forced use of natural science to warrant (in the sense of providing a logical or evidential basis for) one's creedal commitments regarding the transcendent realm. We said, for example, that "science held hostage to any ideology or belief system, whether naturalistic or theistic, can no longer function effectively to gain knowledge of the physical universe.

When the epistemic goal of gaining knowledge is replaced by the dogmatic goal of providing warrant for one's personal belief system or for some sectarian creed, the superficial activity that remains may no longer be called natural science. It may be termed *world view warranting* or *creed confirmation,* or one may put it into the category of *folk science,* but it no longer deserves the label of *natural science"* (pp. 41-42).

Picking up on that reference to folk science, we referred in our closing remarks of chapter eight to *creation science* as an example of special creationist folk science, and to Atkins's *The Creation* as an illustration of naturalistic folk science. In this epilogue, then, let us reflect briefly on how this concept of folk science can provide us with fruitful insights into both scientific creationism and evolutionary naturalism—the principals in the contemporary creation-evolution debate.

Folk Sciences and the Creation-Evolution Debate

The distinction between professional natural science and the various strains of folk science is an important one. As defined by conventional practice and exemplified by the professional scientific literature, natural science ordinarily strives to be blind to religious and ideological commitments in its assessment of scientific theories. Self-consciously restricting itself to the domain of the inherent intelligibility of the physical universe, natural science chooses to remain silent on questions concerning the relationship of the material world to other realms of being.

A characteristic property of folk science, however, is its use of knowledge about the material world (whether accurate or not, or whether gained by common experience, amateur science or professional science is irrelevant) for the purpose of confirming a world view—a set of beliefs which provide a stable framework for dealing with the world of experience in a confident and satisfying manner. One's folk science is an integral component of one's world view, and virtually everyone has a folk science of one sort or another.

Folk science is to be recognized, not necessarily eliminated. Those of us who are educators ought to recognize folk science as serving a function very different from that of professional natural science. The goal of the natural sciences is to gain knowledge concerning the physical world, irrespective of its place in the larger Universe of reality. The incorporation of that knowledge into a comprehensive world view which specifies the existence, character and relative status of God, humankind and the physical universe would be the function of one's folk science.

The contemporary creation-evolution debate may be understood as a shouting match between two competing folk sciences. As the debate is most commonly conducted, the two contenders are evolutionary naturalism and scientific creationism. Evolutionary naturalism is a folk science which seeks to employ the scientific concept of evolutionary development as a warrant for its nontheistic world view. Scientific creationism is a folk science which claims scientific evidence for its scenario of a recent creation by divine fiat. The debate, therefore, is not a contest between natural science and religious belief. It is a confrontation of two folk sciences, each seeking to employ the results of scientific investigation in the support of its own world view.

A portion of that debate—that portion concerned with the analysis of empirical data and the assessment of scientific theories—may fall within the domain of natural science. Questions concerning the duration of cosmic history, the interpretation of the geological record, the temporal succession of life forms, the physical mechanisms required for evolutionary development and like questions are suitable topics for discussion within the context of a science classroom.

We must, however, distinguish these authentically scientific questions from the religious questions which lie at the heart of the folk-science debate and generate most of its emotional energy. The assessment of theories or data relevant to natural science must be distinguished from the evaluation of the creedal assertions of either naturalism or creationism. What is the key to this distinction? Perhaps the most revealing and critical test is to examine the domain, or scope, of a particular statement (or theory, question, speculation, assertion). Is it concerned only with the inherent intelligibility of the physical universe? Is its domain of concern restricted to the properties, behavior or temporal development of material systems irrespective of the existence or activity of nonphysical beings? If so, it is a matter for scientific investigation.

On the other hand, is its principal concern the relationship of the physical world with other realms of being? Does it, for example, function either to confirm or to deny the existence and action of deity? Does its domain of concern include questions about the status of the physical universe relative to deity? Is it concerned with the implications of that status for matters pertaining to the origin, governance, value or purpose of the universe? If so, it is not an appropriate matter for scientific investigation.

Questions concerning the relationship of the physical world to other realms of being are religious and metaphysical questions which must be directed elsewhere—to whatever serves as a person's source of answers to religious questions: parents, cultural traditions, religious institutions, the Bible, classical literature, philosophical speculation, and the like. These are very important questions, and they deserve appropriate consideration. But to be treated adequately they must be clearly distinguished from the more restricted questions that fall within the limited domain of natural science. One of the tragedies of the contemporary creation-evolution debate is, in our judgment, the failure to distinguish questions of inherent intelligibility from questions of external relationship, the failure to distinguish scientific matters from religious matters, the failure to distinguish natural science from folk science.

Evaluating Scientific Creationism as Folk Science

In the second part of this book we presented several case studies under the heading: "Science Indentured to Creationism." What do these case studies illustrate? In our judgment, each of these critiques functions as a vivid illustration of a scientific-creationist folk science in action.

As a folk science, scientific creationism is concerned to use its perception of the physical world for the purpose of warranting certain creedal commitments. Chief among the creedal propositions to be confirmed by the results of scientific-creationist investigation is a scenario for cosmic history which requires the recent inception (6,000-10,000 years ago) of a mature and fully functioning universe having structure and contents essentially the same as we see at the present moment, except for the geological changes caused by a global flood.

In order to produce results that conform to such severe constraints, creation science must operate in a manner quite different from professional natural science. To be more specific, we believe that our case studies have forcefully documented serious failures of creation science to honor the laudable system of values that are characteristic of the professional scientific community.

Rather than reciting here a list of such failures, we invite readers to evaluate the scientific adequacy of the evidence, arguments and conclusions offered by creation scientists in support of a recent inception of the universe. Employing the value system developed in chapter two, the following questions are especially relevant: (1) Is the claim in question based on empirical investigation or theoretical argumentation that is marked by the appropriate level of craft competence? (2) When data are reported, or when extrapolations beyond the data are offered, is professional integrity being maintained in the manner expected by the scientific community? (3) When theories are being evaluated, is the system of epistemic values being employed in an appropriate manner? Or, on the other hand, has the normal epistemic value system been replaced by another criterion, such as conformity to a position already firmly established by means other than scientific investigation?

On the basis of case studies such as we have presented in the second part of this book, we believe that creation science scores poorly on all three of the above questions. Judged as natural science, the evidences and models offered by the scientific-creationist community fail the test of scientific adequacy.

Why is this the case? What has led to this particular state of affairs? The thesis we offer is this: Because scientific creationism functions principally as a folk science, its concern for matters of craft competence, professional integrity and epistemic values must be given a secondary status relative to the primary goal of providing a scientifically naive community with reassurance that its recent-creation scenario is credible. Its role is not to discover answers to open-ended questions, but to provide the appearance of scientific warrant for answers already established by other means.

Because the answers that creation science seeks to warrant are so closely related to a set of religious beliefs, it has often been suggested that creation science should be categorized as religion rather than as science. While there may be some merit to that suggestion, we judge it more accurate and helpful to classify it as a folk science for which particular beliefs about the physical universe—especially about its formative history—are integral components of a religion-centered tradition.

Once this folk-science identification is recognized, critics are free to evaluate the scientific issues quite independent of the genuinely religious questions, which together comprise the scientific-creationist position. Each of the authors of this book, for example, is wholly committed to the Christian faith, firmly believing that God and the physical universe are related in a way that is profoundly portrayed by the Creator-Creation metaphor. Yet we are also convinced of the scientific inadequacy of the scientific-creationist perspective.

The concept of creation is, we believe, a thoroughly religious matter concerning the identities and interrelationships of God, humanity and the physical world. Furthermore, we judge that the scientific question concerning the physical character and chronology of cosmic history belongs in a distinctly different category and deserves open-ended investigation on its own merits. As whole persons, however, we do seek to integrate these religious and scientific concerns into a single coherent world view. In that genuinely human enterprise we place a high value on both candor and integrity.

Evaluating Evolutionary Naturalism as Folk Science

Our chapter reviewing Atkins's *The Creation* concluded by identifying that book as an exemplar of naturalistic folk science. Reaching that conclusion required no extraordinary insight, however.

Already in the preface Atkins made it clear that his principal aim was to demonstrate, presumably by scientific argumentation alone, that the world's existence and patterned behavior require no Supreme Being. But questions concerning the necessity or non-necessity of a Divine Source for the world's existence or of a Divine Governor for the physical behavior of the universe lie well outside of the domain of natural science. The subject matter of such questions is clearly metaphysical, with profound religious significance. Thus, because the principal question treated in *The Creation* is the metaphysical-religious question of the relationship of the physical universe to a transcendent deity (which Atkins argues does not exist) this book cannot be identified or evaluated as natural science or the product of scientific theorizing alone.

But is it folk science? Indeed it is. It has a definite creedal perspective. It clearly advocates reductive materialism or evolutionary naturalism. But even more to the point, *The Creation* seeks to use the scientific concept of cosmic evolution to provide warrant for that naturalistic creed. It seeks passionately to indenture the results of professional natural science in the service of warranting a metaphysical-religious commitment already in place. We must conclude, therefore, that *The Creation* is an exemplar of the folk science of evolutionary naturalism. This is the category to which it belongs, and any critical assessment of it must begin with that recognition.

Similar comments apply to Sagan's "Cosmos" television series. The results of natural science were presented not simply as the content of a lesson in science education, but as the evidential basis for a naturalistic religious world view. "Cosmos" was naturalistic folk science in a remarkably provocative and effective form. Its principal agenda was thoroughly religious: to imply that a naturalistic world view is warranted by natural science, to declare naturalism the victor over theism and to inspire a sense of identity and purpose rooted in religious loyalty to the universe itself. Although the forms of religious theater found in "Cosmos" may have been more subtle than what one finds in a fundamentalist revival tent, its evangelistic fervor was nonetheless intense.

As we did in the case of special creationist folk science, we invite the reader to perform a critical evaluation of Atkins's *The Creation,* Sagan's "Cosmos" or any other representative specimen of naturalistic folk science. Because evolutionary naturalism seeks to base its perception of the physical universe firmly on the results of professional natural science, we find relatively few occasions to complain about shortcomings in the areas of craft competence, professional integrity or the employment of an appropriate set of epistemic values. The normal functioning of the professional scientific community provides, we believe, an adequate amount of self-discipline in these matters. However, our chief concern here is to note what we judge to be serious violations of the boundaries of the scientific domain and a general failure to honor certain very important distinctions.

How can naturalistic folk science be distinguished from authentic natural science in the popular literature? We suggest that the following three questions be addressed to the literature under scrutiny:

1. What categories of questions are of principal concern? If a particular discussion is carefully limited to questions regarding the inherent intelligibility of the physical universe and its constituent parts, it is functioning solidly within the restricted domain of natural science.

But if, on the other hand, the principal concerns include some of the basic tenets of naturalism—no deity, no divine action in the world, no transcendent source of value or purpose—the material is likely to be naturalistic folk science.

As a folk science, evolutionary naturalism seeks to employ the scientific concept of evolution to warrant its creed. In some instances this may be accomplished in a rather subtle manner simply by basing the whole discussion on the unstated, but nonetheless effective, presupposition that there is no significant distinction between natural science and evolutionary naturalism. Much of Sagan's "Cosmos," we judge, follows this strategy. In such a context, any discussion of the relevant metaphysical-religious issues is likely to be infrequent or superficial. Atkins's book, on the other hand, is very up-front about its agenda. From the beginning, its anti-theistic agenda is stated explicitly so that there need be no doubt whatsoever concerning its identity as folk-science literature written for persons who wish to believe that their evolutionary naturalism has the blessing of the prestigious professional scientific community.

2. Is the distinction between origin *and* formation *made clear?* As we discussed in chapter one, natural science can fruitfully investigate the formation of various structures within the physical world, but it is incapable of dealing with the ultimate origin of existence, which is, once again, a metaphysical-religious matter. Discussions of cosmic evolution which overlook this formation-origin distinction are likely to function principally as folk science. Without this distinction, any reconstruction of the formative history of the universe tends to function as a "story of origins" in the sense of an explanation of existence itself.

In *The Creation* Atkins is very candid in his claim that we are on the verge of scientifically understanding how this awesome universe could create itself from "absolutely nothing." (What he calls by the name *absolutely nothing*, however, appears to be some nonphysical entity that possesses the capability of self-transformation into this physical universe. Even self-creating universes, it seems, must begin with some form of "self.") Once again, *The Creation* reveals its folk-science identity.

3. Is the distinction between behavior *and* governance *made clear?* In the absence of a clear delineation of the difference between the scientific description of a thing's *behavior* and the identification of the source of the *governance* of that behavior, natural science is likely to be perceived as if it were a competitor to any theistic perspective. The concept of the "natural" behavior of a physical system would then function as a rival to the concept of divine governance.

In the folk-science literature of evolutionary naturalism, for example, the functioning assumption is that if there is a scientific description (or theory) of the processes involved in the formation of species, then there is no room for a theistic concept of the divine governance of those processes. Readers are led, sometimes openly, sometimes surreptitiously, to adopt an either-or stance: The phenomena that comprise cosmic formation happen *either* as "natural" processes (scientifically describable) *or* as consequences of divine action. Once this "either-or-manship" is in place, then even a scientifically informed reconstruction of the formative history of the universe functions as naturalistic folk science, reassuring all of those persons who wish to believe that the scientific concept of evolution provides warrant for their naturalistic interpretation of physical phenomena.

We hope that the case studies and other discussions in this volume will be helpful in clarifying the character of natural science as presently practiced, and in distinguishing it from two particular strains of folk science that function in contemporary culture. Science, folk science and religion each occupy a legitimate place in the human enterprise, but great mischief is done when their differences go unrecognized. Surely the resurgent creation-evolution debate provides ample evidence for that.

Notes

Introduction: Charting the Course
[1]The historically fruitful partnership of natural science and the Christian faith has been documented by numerous writers. Highly readable accounts can be found in the following recent publications: Charles E. Hummel, *The Galileo Connection: Resolving Conflicts between Science & the Bible* (Downers Grove, Ill.: InterVarsity Press, 1986); David N. Livingstone, *Darwin's Forgotten Defenders: The Encounter between Evangelical Theology and Evolutionary Thought* (Grand Rapids: Eerdmans, 1987); and Colin A. Russell, *Crosscurrents: Interactions between Science & Faith* (Grand Rapids: Eerdmans, 1985).

Chapter 1: Locating the Boundary
[1]See Carl Sagan, *Cosmos* (New York: Random House, 1980), p. 4.
[2]Donald M. Mackay, *The Clockwork Image* (Downers Grove, Ill.: InterVarsity Press, 1974).
[3]If the reader is not well acquainted with the application of the natural sciences to the study of formative history, it may be helpful to consult an introductory textbook in earth science, or geology, or astronomy. Such textbooks ordinarily include a discussion of the ways in which the formative history of the earth or of stars is scientifically investigated.
[4]A similar delineation of the domain of natural science can be found in Howard J.

Van Till, *The Fourth Day: What the Bible and the Heavens Are Telling Us about the Creation* (Grand Rapids: Eerdmans, 1986), especially chapters six and ten.

Chapter 2: The Path Most Traveled

[1]See, for example, the following: Thomas S. Kuhn, *The Structure of Scientific Revolutions*, 2d ed. (Chicago: University of Chicago Press, 1970), and *The Essential Tension* (Chicago: University of Chicago Press, 1977), especially chapter thirteen, "Objectivity, Value Judgment, and Theory Choice," pp. 320-39; Larry Laudan, *Science and Values* (Berkeley: University of California Press, 1984); Ernan McMullin, "Values in Science," *PSA 1982* [Proceedings of the 1982 biennial meeting of the Philosophy of Science Association] (E. Lansing, Mich.: Philosophy of Science Association, 1983), Vol. 2; and Jerome R. Ravetz, *Scientific Knowledge and Its Social Problems* (New York: Oxford University Press, 1971).

[2]Our thanks to Professor Robert E. Snow for suggesting this set of four categories.

[3]Ernan McMullin, "Values in Science," pp. 1-25. For other discussions of scientific-theory evaluation, see W. H. Newton-Smith, *The Rationality of Science* (Boston: Routledge and Kegan Paul, 1981), pp. 226-32; Thomas S. Kuhn, *The Essential Tension* (Chicago: University of Chicago Press, 1977), pp. 320-39; and Del Ratzsch, *Philosophy of Science: The Natural Sciences in Christian Perspective* (Downers Grove, Ill.: InterVarsity Press, 1986), pp. 75-96.

[4]See Paul Davies, *Superforce* (New York: Simon and Schuster, 1984).

[5]We are using the term *folk science* in a manner similar to that of Jerome R. Ravetz in *Scientific Knowledge and Its Social Problems* (New York: Oxford University Press, 1971), especially pp. 386-97. Ravetz defines *folk science* as that "part of a general world-view, or ideology, which is given special articulation so that it may provide comfort and reassurance in the face of the crucial uncertainties of the world of experience" (p. 386).

[6]For a brief typology of positions on this question, see Ratzsch, *Philosophy of Science*, pp. 141-48.

Chapter 3: The Legend of the Shrinking Sun

[1]J. A. Eddy and A. A. Boornazian, "Secular Decrease in the Solar Diameter, 1836-1953," *Bulletin of the American Astronomical Society* 11 (1979):437. Note: this is only an abstract. The full text was never published.

[2]G. B. Lubkin, "Analyses of Historical Data Suggest Sun Is Shrinking," *Physics Today* 32, No. 9 (1979):17. The reference to the 1567 solar eclipse does not appear in the abstract (ref. 1), but can be found in this news report regarding Eddy and Boornazian's presentation.

[3]See the comments by Martin Schwarzschild reported in ref. 2. For an extensive review article which discusses these matters, see Gordon Newkirk, Jr., "Variations in Solar Luminosity," *Annual Review of Astronomy and Astrophysics*, 21 (1983):429-67.

[4]S. Sofia, J. O'Keefe, J. R. Lesh, and A. S. Endal, "Solar Constant: Constraints on Possible Variations Derived from Solar Diameter Measurements," *Science* 204 (1979):1306.

[5]Irwin I. Shapiro, "Is the Sun Shrinking?" *Science* 208 (1980):51.

[6]D. W. Dunham, S. Sofia, A. D. Fiala, D. Herald and P. M. Muller, "Observations of

a Probable Change in the Solar Radius between 1715 and 1979," *Science* 210 (1980):1243.

[7]J. H. Parkinson, L. V. Morrison and F. R. Stephenson, "The constancy of the solar diameter over the past 250 years," *Nature* 288 (1980):548.

[8]R. L. Gilliland, "Solar Radius Variations over the Past 264 Years," *Astrophysical Journal* 248 (1981):1144.

[9]J. H. Parkinson, "New Measurements of the Solar Diameter," *Nature* 304 (1983):518.

[10]S. Sofia, D. W. Dunham, J. B. Dunham and A. D. Fiala, "Solar Radius Change between 1925 and 1979," *Nature* 304 (1983):522.

[11]C. Frohlich and J. A. Eddy, "Observed Relation between Solar Luminosity and Radius" [a paper presented at an international conference sponsored by the Committee on Space Research, July 1984 in Graz, Austria].

[12]Russell Akridge, "The Sun Is Shrinking," *Impact* No. 82 (Institute for Creation Research, April 1980), pp. iii, iv.

[13]See Thomas G. Barnes, "Evidence Points to a Recent Creation," *Christianity Today*, October 8, 1982, pp. 34-36.

[14]See *ORIGINS Film Series Handbook* (Phoenix, Ariz.: Films for Christ Association, 1983), pp. 11-12.

[15]In order to give due recognition to an important symmetry, we should note that just as scientific creationism functions as the folk science of contemporary Christian fundamentalism, so also naturalistic evolutionism functions as the folk science of modern Western naturalism. In each case, selected results of scientific investigation are interpreted in such a way that they may be employed to bolster a creedal tenet of a world view or ideology.

[16]Walter T. Brown, Jr., "The Scientific Case for Creation," *Bible-Science Newsletter*, July, 1984, p. 14.

[17]Henry M. Morris, *The Biblical Basis of Modern Science* (Grand Rapids: Baker Book House, 1984), p. 164.

[18]Hilton Hinderliter, "The Shrinking Sun: A Creationist's Prediction, Its Verification, and the Resulting Implications for Theories of Origins," *Creation Research Society Quarterly* 17 (1980):57; "The Inconsistent Sun: How Has It Been Behaving, and What Might It Do Next?" *Creation Research Society Quarterly* 17 (1980):143.

[19]See Lubkin, "Analyses."

[20]See Newkirk, "Variations."

[21]Hinderliter, "The Shrinking Sun," p. 57.

[22]Ibid., p. 59.

[23]Ibid.

[24]See Chapter IV, "Stellar Evolution and Nucleosynthesis," in *A Source Book in Astronomy and Astrophysics, 1900-1975*, edited by Kenneth R. Lang and Owen Gingerich (Cambridge, Mass.: Harvard University Press, 1979). This collection of original papers and editorial commentary provides an excellent overview of this important episode in the history of astrophysics.

[25]Hinderliter, "The Shrinking Sun," p. 59.

[26]James Hanson, "The Sun's Luminosity and Age," *Creation Research Society Quarterly* 18 (1981):27.

[27]See refs. 4 and 5.

[28]Hanson, "The Sun's Luminosity and Age," p. 29.

[29]Ibid.

[30]Paul M. Steidl, "Solar Neutrinos and a Young Sun," *Creation Research Society Quarterly* 17 (1980):63.

[31]Ibid., p. 60.

[32]Ibid., p. 64.

[33]Paul M. Steidl, "Recent Developments about Solar Neutrinos," (Letter) *Creation Research Society Quarterly* 17 (1981):233.

[34]Howard J. Van Till, "The Legend of the Shrinking Sun," *Journal of the American Scientific Affiliation* 38, No. 3 (1986), pp. 164-74.

[35]Thomas G. Barnes, "The Dilemma of a Theistic Evolutionist: An Answer to Howard Van Till," *Creation Research Society Quarterly* 23 (1987):167-71.

Chapter 4: Footprints on the Dusty Moon

[1]For a well-written and well-illustrated report on this historic landing, see *National Geographic Magazine*, December 1969, pp. 738 ff.

[2]Ibid., p. 736.

[3]Walter T. Brown, Jr., *Evidence that Implies a Young Earth and Solar System* (Naperville, Ill.: ICR Midwest, 1981).

[4]*ORIGINS Film Series Handbook* (Phoenix, Ariz.: Films for Christ Association, 1983), p. 13.

[5]John D. Buddhue, *Meteoritic Dust* (Albuquerque: University of New Mexico Press, 1950).

[6]F. G. Watson, *Between the Planets* (Cambridge, Mass.: Harvard University Press, 1956).

[7]E. J. Opik, "Interplanetary Dust and Terrestrial Accretion of Meteoritic Matter," *Irish Astronomical Journal* 4 (1956):84-135.

[8]Fred L. Whipple, "On the Lunar Dust Layer" in *Vistas in Astronautics*, vol. 2 (New York: Pergamon Press, 1959).

[9]Hans Petterson, "Cosmic Spherules and Meteoritic Dust," *Scientific American* 202 (Feb. 1960):123-32.

[10]Gerald S. Hawkins, ed., *Meteor Orbits and Dust: The Proceedings of a Symposium* (Washington, D.C.: NASA Publication SP-135, 1967), and *Smithsonian Contributions to Astrophysics* 11 (1967).

[11]C. S. Nilsson, "Some Doubts about the Earth's Dust Cloud," *Science* 153 (1966):1242-46.

[12]Donald E. Gault, et al., "Effects of Microcratering on the Lunar Surface," *Proceedings of the Third Lunar Science Conference* (Cambridge, Mass.: MIT Press, 1972), pp. 2713-34.

[13]G. Field and A. G. W. Cameron, eds., *The Dusty Universe* (New York: Smithsonian Astrophysical Observatory, 1973), p. 191.

[14]J. A. M. McDonnell, ed., *Cosmic Dust* (New York: John Wiley and Sons, 1978), pp. 150-57.

[15]R. B. Baldwin, *The Face of the Moon* (Chicago: University of Chicago Press, 1949).

[16]R. A. Lyttleton, *The Modern Universe* (New York: Harper & Brothers, 1956).

[17]Ibid., p. 72.

[18]Thomas Gold, "The Lunar Surface," *Monthly Notices of the Royal Astronomical Society*, 115 (1955):585.

[19]Whipple, "Lunar Dust Layer."

[20]J. W. Salisbury and V. G. Smalley, "The Lunar Surface Layer," in Salisbury and Glaser, eds., *The Lunar Surface Layer* (New York: Academic Press, 1964).

[21]Stuart Ross Taylor, *Lunar Science: A Post-Apollo View* (New York: Pergamon Press, 1975).

[22]*Apollo-17 Preliminary Science Report* (Washington, D.C.: NASA Publication SP-330, 1973).

[23]See Taylor, *Lunar Science.*

[24]Harold S. Slusher, "Some Astronomical Evidences for a Youthful Solar System," *Creation Research Society Quarterly* 8 (1971):55.

[25]Brown, *Evidence.*

[26]*Observing God's World* (Pensacola, Fla.: A Beka Book Publications, 1978), p. 76.

[27]Henry M. Morris, ed., *Scientific Creationism* (San Diego: Creation-Life Publishers, 1974), pp. 151-52.

[28]Gault, "Effects of Microcratering."

[29]Taylor, *Lunar Science.*

Chapter 5: Timeless Tales from the Salty Sea

[1]John Joly, "An Estimate of the Geological Age of the Earth," in *Smithsonian Institution Annual Report* for the year ending June 30, 1899 (Washington, D.C.: Government Printing Office, 1901), pp. 247-88.

[2]J. P. Riley and G. Skirrow, eds., *Chemical Oceanography* (New York: Academic Press, 1965). See especially chapter five, "Minor Elements in Sea Water," by Edward D. Goldberg.

[3]Henry M. Morris, ed., *Scientific Creationism* (San Diego: Creation-Life Publishers, 1974), p. 154.

[4]Ibid., p. 153.

[5]Ibid., p. 154.

[6]John C. Whitcomb, Jr., and Henry M. Morris, *The Genesis Flood* (Philadelphia: Presbyterian and Reformed Publishing Co., 1962); Henry M. Morris and Gary E. Parker, *What Is Creation Science?* (San Diego: Creation-Life Publishers, 1982); Henry M. Morris, *The Biblical Basis for Modern Science* (Grand Rapids: Baker Book House, 1984); Walter T. Brown, Jr., "The Scientific Case for Creation," *Bible-Science Newsletter*, June, July and August, 1984.

[7]Melvin A. Cook, *Prehistory and Earth Models* (London: Max Parrish, 1966), p. 73.

[8]Morris, *Scientific Creationism*, pp. 154-55.

[9]Ph. H. Kuenen, "Geological Conditions of Sedimentation," in J. P. Riley and G. Skirrow, eds., *Chemical Oceanography* (New York: Academic Press, 1965), chap. 14.

[10]Kenneth Hsu, "When the Mediterranean Dried Up," *Scientific American* 227 (Dec. 1972):26-36.

[11]Morris, *The Biblical Basis for Modern Science*, pp. 477-80.

[12]See Hildegarde Hawthorne, *Matthew Fontaine Maury, Trail Maker of the Seas* (New York: Longmans, Green and Co., 1943).

[13]*Report on the Scientific Results of the Voyage of H.M.S. "Challenger": Physics and Chemistry*, Vol. 1, part 1 (Edinburgh: Her Majesty's Stationery Office, 1884).

[14]H. U. Sverdrup, M. W. Johnson, and R. H. Fleming, *The Oceans, Their Physics, Chemistry and General Biology* (Englewood Cliffs, N.J.: Prentice-Hall, 1942).

[15]V. M. Goldschmidt, *Geochemistry* (New York: Oxford University Press, 1954).

[16]*Continents Adrift,* a collection of *Scientific American* reprints (San Francisco: Freeman Books, 1972).

[17]J. P. Riley and R. Chester, eds., *Chemical Oceanography,* 2nd ed. (New York: Academic Press, 1975). See especially chapter 33, "The Mineralogy and Chemistry of Near-Shore Sediments," by S. E. Calvert, and chapter 34, "The Geochemistry of Deep-Sea Sediments," by R. Chester and S. R. Astron.

[18]James I. Drever, *The Geochemistry of Natural Waters* (Englewood Cliffs, N.J.: Prentice-Hall, 1982).

[19]Keith Stowe, *Ocean Science* (New York: John Wiley and Sons, 1983).

[20]Ferren MacIntyre, "Why the Sea Is Salt," *Scientific American* 223 (November 1970):104-15.

[21]Robert J. Strutt (Lord Rayleigh), "On the Radioactive Minerals," *Proceedings of the Royal Society of London,* A 76 (Feb. 28, 1905):88-101; Bertram B. Boltwood, "On the Ultimate Disintegration of the Radioactive Elements; Part II, The Disintegration Products of Uranium," *American Journal of Science* 23 (Feb., 1907):77-88; Arthur Holmes, "The Association of Lead with Uranium in Rock Minerals, and Its Application to the Measurement of Geological Time," *Proceedings of the Royal Society of London* 85 (Mar. 20, 1911):248-56.

Chapter 6: Making Mysteries out of Missing Rock

[1]Walter Lang, *Geological Study Course on Grand Canyon Arizona,* p. 31. Available from the Bible-Science Association, 2911 E. 42nd St., Minneapolis, Minn.

[2]For a summary paper with an extensive list of references on the geology of the Canyon, see Edwin D. McKee, "Stratified Rocks of the Grand Canyon," U.S. Geological Survey Professional Paper 669-B, 1969, pp. 23-58.

[3]The names of formations of layered rocks are generally derived from localities where those particular formations are especially well exposed. For example, the Moenkopi Formation is named after Moenkopi, Arizona. Some of the names of formations in the Grand Canyon are derived from prominent features within the Canyon; for example, Vishnu Schist after the Vishnu Temple.

The standard geological periods have been named after localities (Pennsylvanian, Devonian), tribes of people (Silurian and Ordovician after ancient Welsh tribes), characteristic rock type (Cretaceous from creta, Latin for chalk) and relative position (Tertiary). Rocks are assigned to the appropriate geological period on the bases of characteristic fossil remains, by which they can ordinarily be identified, and their position relative to rocks belonging to other periods. The criterion of relative position succeeds because in stacks of undisturbed layered rocks around the world, rocks of younger age are invariably found overlying rocks of older age. For example, Triassic rocks always overlie Permian or older rocks, and Mississippian rocks always underlie Permian or younger rocks unless a great disturbance has overturned the rocks.

The dating of geological-period boundaries is a matter of constant discussion among geologists, and not all geologists are likely to agree on the exact same set of values. The ages used in figure 3 have been taken from one of the most recent evaluations of the geologic time scale, namely, W. B. Harland, *A Geologic Time Scale* (Cambridge: Cambridge University Press, 1982), p. 4-5.

[4]Some geologists have also suggested the designation Nankoweap Group for some of

the layered rocks between the Unkar and Chuar Groups.

[5]Igneous rocks are those that have solidified either underground or on the earth's surface from previously molten rock. Metamorphic rocks are those that have been recrystallized well below the earth's surface under the influence of extremely high pressures and temperatures. Before metamorphism, such rocks may have been igneous, metamorphic or some kind of sedimentary rock such as shale, limestone or sandstone.

[6]The Ordovician and Silurian periods follow the Cambrian and come before the Devonian (see figure 3).

[7]A summary diagram of a creationist flood model can be seen in *Bible-Science Newsletter*, 15 (1977):5.

[8]Lang, *Geological Study Course*, and Clifford L. Burdick, *The Canyon of Canyons* (Minneapolis: Bible-Science Association, 1974).

[9]Lang, *Geological Study Course*, p. 6; Burdick, *Canyon of Canyons*, pp. 60-61.

[10]Here the term *kinds* is used in the sense of the "kinds" of Genesis 1 as translated from the Hebrew word *min*.

[11]Burdick, *Canyon of Canyons*, pp. 27, 59-60.

[12]Ibid., pp. 65-74.

[13]Ibid., pp. 41-51; Lang, *Geological Study Course*, pp. 4-5.

[14]"Grand Canyon 'Creation' Story," *Bible-Science Newsletter*, 14 (1976):1.

[15]Gary E. Parker, *Creation: the Facts of Life* (San Diego: CLP, 1980), pp. 123-4.

[16]"Grand Canyon Presents Problems for Long Ages," in *Bible-Science Newsletter* (an insert under the heading, "Five Minutes with the Bible & Science") 18 (1980):4.

[17]"A New Look at Arizona's Grand Canyon," in *Bible-Science Newsletter* (an insert under the heading, "Five Minutes with the Bible & Science") 20 (1982):1.

[18]"Grand Canyon Presents Problems for Long Ages," p. 8.

[19]Robert P. Sharp, "Ep-Archean and Ep-Algonkian Erosion Surfaces, Grand Canyon, Arizona," *Geological Society of America Bulletin*, 51 (1940):1235-70. See specifically a photograph on plate 4, figure 1, facing p. 1244 in Sharp's paper.

[20]Ibid., p. 1244.

[21]Ibid., p. 1245.

[22]Ibid., p. 1248.

[23]Ibid., p. 1252.

[24]*Archean* is a term that refers to the earth's very oldest rocks. These are typically, though not exclusively, igneous and metamorphic rocks that can ultimately be found beneath the layered sedimentary rocks that characterize most of the earth's surface.

[25]Sharp, "Ep-Archean and Ep-Algonkian Erosion Surfaces," p. 1261.

[26]Burdick, *Canyon of Canyons*, p. 3.

[27]E. D. McKee and R. C. Gutschick, *History of the Redwall Limestone of Northern Arizona* (Boulder: Geological Society of America, 1969).

[28]Ibid., pp. 22-23.

[29]Ibid., p. 16.

[30]Ibid., p. 18.

[31]Ibid., p. 21.

[32]Andrew H. McNair, "Paleozoic Stratigraphy of Part of Northwestern Arizona," *American Association of Petroleum Geologists Bulletin*, 35 (1951): 503-41. McNair measured 216

feet of predominantly limestone in the Virgin Mountains of easternmost Nevada and tentatively assigned the rocks to the Pogonip Limestone of probably Ordovician age. McNair also measured in the Virgin Mountains 651 feet of Cambrian Limestone that overlies the Peasley Limestone, the western lateral equivalent of the Muav. As indicated from sections measured east of the Virgin Mountains, these post-Muav Cambrian Limestones thinned eastward.

[33]Burdick, *Canyon of Canyons*, p. 77.

[34]Charles B. Hunt, "Geologic History of the Colorado River," U.S. Geological Survey Professional Paper 669-C, 1969, p. 65.

[35]"Grand Canyon Presents Problems for Long Ages," p. 4.

[36]Edwin D. McKee, "The Supai Group of Grand Canyon," U.S. Geological Survey Professional Paper 1173, 1982, p. 4.

[37]McKee and Gutschick, *History of the Redwall Limestone*, p. 74. Talus refers to the pile of rocks at the base of a cliff. The rocks were dislodged from the cliff and fell to the base.

[38]See G. H. Billingsley and E. D. McKee, "Pre-Supai Buried Valleys" in McKee, "Supai Group," pp. 137-47.

[39]Ibid., p. 139.

[40]Ibid.

[41]Ibid., p. 190.

[42]Ibid., pp. 155-76.

[43]"Grand Canyon 'Creation' Story," *Bible-Science Newsletter*, v. 14, 1976, p. 1.

[44]Ibid.

[45]The principle of uniformity is one of the most widely discussed and misunderstood principles in geology. Those who wish to understand the term would do well to read Martin J. S. Rudwick, "Uniformity and Progression: Reflections on the Structure of Geological Theory in the Age of Lyell," in D. H. D. Roller, *Perspectives in the History of Science and Technology* (Norman, Okla.: University of Oklahoma, 1971), and also Stephen Jay Gould, "Toward the Vindication of Punctuational Change," in *Catastrophes and Earth History* (Princeton: Princeton University Press, 1984).

[46]The principle of superposition is a fundamental principle of geology in which it is stated simply that in any succession of layered rocks that has not been overturned or injected by parallel sheets of igneous rock, the layer at the bottom of the succession was deposited first and succeeding layers were deposited sequentially.

[47]For example, radiometric dating of a variety of rocks and minerals using several well-established techniques repeatedly discloses that earth materials typically have ages measurable in terms of a few million to a few billion years in age. Indeed, one lava flow in the western end of the Grand Canyon that clearly erupted after all the layered sedimentary rocks were deposited has been dated by Potassium-argon dating as about 1.2 million years old. Clearly the theory of a global flood that occurred only a few thousand years ago is incompatible with such an age for the lava flow. Moreover, all the layered rocks, since they underlie the lava flow, must be older than 1.2 million years.

Biogeography concerns the distribution of plants and animals over the face of the earth. That distribution is totally at odds with the theory of a global flood and the preservation of animals on Noah's ark. As one example, consider the fact that all fossil sloths occur in the rocks of the Americas. During a global flood all sloths would inevitably be drowned and therefore would become extinct. Sloths are extremely slow movers and could never be expected to flee to high ground during a flood. If they were to be preserved by having them board Noah's ark, then several sloths would have to migrate to the Middle East.

That, of course, is rather unlikely since sloths, as arboreal animals, don't like to move more than a few feet to find water or get from one tree to another. Also, three-toed sloths eat nothing but Cecropia tree leaves, a treat they would be unlikely to find all the way to Noah's ark. Then the problem is compounded by the need to have the sloths migrate all the way back to South America at the conclusion of the flood since that is the only place they live today. The problem could be multiplied a thousandfold by considering the improbabilities of the migration of Australian marsupials to the ark, or the difficulties of preserving river dolphins, freshwater fish, snakes and turtles and so on.

Chapter 7: Popular Portraits of Science: Focused or Fuzzy?

[1]In spite of the fact that many within the scientific-creationist movement who are actively involved in writing in defense of scientific creationism have Ph.D. degrees in science, it is very difficult to regard these people as professional, practicing scientists. They do not demonstrate the marks of integrity that are so important in professional science (see, for example, the case studies of part two), and most of them are not actively practicing in a field of science by conducting legitimate research following the accepted canons of scientific practice.

[2]For P. W. Atkins, see our chapter eight. Carl Sagan's *Cosmos* begins with the overtly naturalistic statement, "The cosmos is all that is or ever was or ever will be." One wonders how Sagan can know that.

[3]These works do, however, criticize specific religious tenets when they masquerade as science. For example, the scientific-creationist claim that scientific evidence supports the notion of special creation of organisms is attacked by these evolutionists because it is a scientific claim as well as a religious one.

[4]Niles Eldredge, *The Monkey Business* (New York: Washington Square, 1982); Norman D. Newell, *Creation and Evolution* (New York: Columbia University Press, 1982); Philip Kitcher, *Abusing Science* (Cambridge, Mass.: MIT Press, 1982); and Michael Ruse, *Darwinism Defended* (Reading, Mass.: Addison-Wesley, 1982).

[5]Eldredge, *The Monkey Business,* p. 18.

[6]Ibid.

[7]Michael Ruse, for example, has an entire chapter devoted to evolution and ethics in his *Darwinism Defended.* In that chapter he takes great pains to dismiss evolutionary ethics and social Darwinism.

[8]Kitcher, *Abusing Science,* p. 200.

[9]Isaac Asimov, *In the Beginning* (New York: Crown, 1981).

[10]Douglas J. Futuyma, *Science on Trial* (New York: Pantheon, 1983).

[11]See our chapter one for a brief discussion of the term *scientism.*

[12]According to Asimov, his book "merely considers the verse of the Bible, line by line and, indeed, word by word, discusses the content and meaning and compares them with the scientific view that pertains to the passage" (p. 2).

[13]Henry M. Morris, *The Genesis Record* (San Diego: Creation-Life, 1976).

[14]Asimov's view of the Bible falls far short of an adequate view of Scripture as the Word of God. "The Biblical writers and editors were thoughtful men who borrowed selectively, choosing what they considered good and rejecting what seemed nonsensical or unedifying. They labored to produce something that was as reasonable and as useful as possible" (p. 3).

[15]Asimov, *In the Beginning*, p. 11.

[16]Ibid.

[17]For a satisfying, readable overview of the genuine reactions of scientists in response to the developments of science see, for example, C. A. Russell, *Cross-Currents* (Grand Rapids: Eerdmans, 1985). Many other excellent works on the history of science also make it plain that many outstanding scientists, such as Faraday, Newton, Maxwell, Kelvin and others did not draw the conclusions that Asimov thinks were drawn. Consult, for example, the work of Hooykaas, Klaaren, Raven, Dillenberger and Peacocke. A very readable new work is that of C. E. Hummel, *The Galileo Connection* (Downers Grove, Ill.: InterVarsity Press, 1986).

[18]Asimov, *In the Beginning*, pp. 11-12.

[19]We are not here making any judgment about the validity of Futuyma's case for evolution. Futuyma presents the case for evolution cogently and eloquently, but whether or not evolution is "true" is beside the point of the argument that is being made in this case study.

[20]Futuyma, *Science on Trial*, p. 209.

[21]Ibid., p. 213.

[22]Ibid., p. 167.

[23]Ibid., pp. 169-70.

[24]Ibid., p. 147.

[25]Ibid., pp. 12-13.

[26]Ibid., pp. 98-99.

[27]Christians, of course, also confess that God placed us on earth to be conscientious stewards of his good creation. Though we may use the earth, we must use it responsibly as those who are image-bearers of the living God and as those who have been entrusted with something that ultimately belongs to the Creator.

[28]Futuyma, *Science on Trial*, p. 131.

Chapter 8: A Masquerade of Science

[1]P. W. Atkins, *The Creation* (San Francisco: W. H. Freeman & Company, 1981), p. vii.

[2]Ibid.

[3]Ibid.

[4]Edward R. Harrison, *Cosmology: The Science of the Universe* (Cambridge: Cambridge University Press, 1981), pp. 10-11.

[5]Ibid., p. 100.

[6]Ibid.

[7]Atkins, *Creation*, p. vii.

[8]Ibid., p. 6, emphasis added.

[9]Harrison, *Cosmology*, pp. 107-11.

[10]Ibid., p. viii, emphasis added.

[11]Ibid., p. 127.
[12]Carl Sagan, *Cosmos* (New York: Random House, 1980), p. 4.
[13]Atkins, *Creation*, p. 17.
[14]Ibid., p. 17.
[15]Ibid., p. 115.
[16]Ibid., p. 17.
[17]Ibid., p. 107.
[18]Ibid., p. 111.
[19]Ibid., p. 45.
[20]Ibid., p. 21.
[21]Ibid., p. 23.
[22]Ibid., p. 37.

Chapter 9: Sagan's Cosmos
[1]Carl Sagan, *Cosmos* (New York: Random House, 1980), p. 39; though I refer to the television series, quotations will normally by cited from the published version.
[2]Ibid., p. 131.
[3]Ibid., p. 4.
[4]Ibid.
[5]Ibid., p. 180.
[6]Ibid., p. 127.
[7]Ibid., p. 258.
[8]Ibid., p. 242.
[9]Sagan, "Cosmos," Episode 12, emphasis added.
[10]Sagan, "Cosmos," Episode 10, closing lines.
[11]Sagan, *Cosmos,* p. 176.
[12]Ibid., p. 173-74.
[13]Ibid., p. 174.
[14]Ibid., p. 177.
[15]Ibid., p. 258.
[16]Ibid., p. 257.
[17]Sagan, "Cosmos," Episode 4.
[18]Sagan, *Cosmos,* p. 333.
[19]Ibid., p. 345.
[20]Ibid., p. 250, emphasis added.
[21]Ibid., p. 4.

89834
Sci
v3.18

LINCOLN CHRISTIAN COLLEGE AND SEMINARY 82834

501
V282

3 4711 00177 8655